Appreciating Microworld

notes from the Insecthunter

www.dimagehunter.com

1st Edition – RAW version

Cover design by Choo Meng Foo

Book design by Choo Meng Foo

Printed in the United States of America

First Printing: Sunday, November 25, 2012

ISBN-12 345-6-7898765-4-3

Dedication

To the living dead

Michaeangleo and Davinci

Forward

This is a raw copy which had not gone through the arduous task of proof reading and editing. As such, as writer, I felt liberated that I could immediately share it. I too could take a more relax path in refining it. I seek, therefore, if you find, some grammatical error, be reminded that this is a RAW copy. Thanks for the understanding so I could go further to release my other thoughts. It is excruciatingly agonizing for me to linger too long on the same text, spending years on the same while restraining my other thoughts that is bursting out that need my attention to ink them into text.

Content

Acknowledgement

I am grateful to the following people for their help, inspiration, sarcasm and believing/non-believing in this journey,

Paula, Yee Poh Chun,

Poh Fatt, Catherine Cook, Lindy, Li Sin,

Regu, Eddy, Shuh Fang, Sheng Bu Wei, Sheng Yi Yu, Eric, Pang, Chew, Eng Seng, Joseph.

My ardent friends and supporters, Shashi, Francis, Parry, Manoj, Gupta, Marina Blue, Larry, Priscilla, Sharon, Aaron Tan, Michael Baumgart, Martin LaBar, Urtica, ruslou (on & off), aussiegall and many more friends in the Flickr and FB social networking sites.

Entomologists or wannabe , especially omeuceu, longristra, Gavatron, Matt Bertone, thaptor, Norman Penny, alexwild, Pjtor, Heikki Hippa, Neal Evenhis, Peter Chandler, Chris Thompson, Stephen D. Gaimari and Øivind Gammelmo.

Member of the Zhu Clan, William, Johnny, Bill, Ah Kit, Heng Min, Hsing Ming, Heng Wee, Heng Nong, Heng Tien, Xing Yao, Chong Woon, Chor Kuo and many more members of the clan.

" ... woke up, burning, burning, burning in fire, I will speak the language you understand, what good is language if I have nothing to say, and you heard nothing, nothing at all, how useful is perfect grammar and grammatical structure, if I have nothing to say. Rage!!! Burn the cage of language! Freed. I want to speak!"

Choo Meng Foo

1. Experiencing nature

"I love shooting, I love hunting, but I neither kill nor destroy."

Insecthunter

The Starting point

It was in Inner Mongolia that I saw the beauty of insects and spiders. I was taking a break from my architecture and City planning work. I bought a dSLR, and was pursuing my other passion – photography. I started photography when I was fifteen, shots professionally when I was still studying in the college. The pay was enough to sustain my interest and pay for films and prints. It was a pity there wasn't any degree photographic course in Singapore university. I had to register into Architecture courses instead. However, it turned out to be, for the better, it is a great course! I learned to be creative and the way I see things has changed tremendously.

Bashang is a vast grassland that stretches beyond the horizon as far as my vision could reach. It is breath taking. Staring into such vastness and beyond, I was awed and blanked for a moment. The blankness momentarily erased all materialism and simplified complex human relationship that existed in the cosmopolitan into obscurity. Here was none of the complex urban structures, just a shimmering green receding, receding beyond in the rhythmic sweep of the breeze. I took a deep breath and smelled its freshness, with eyes closed. After a moment, I surveyed the terrain. I began to create mental images, and postulate which vantage point would provide great images. I wanted images that speak of this vastness. I ran up the gentle slope, reached the peak, bent or stretched my knee, scouting for images. As I was composing, focusing, framing and shooting, I began to notice the abundance of huge spiders, about two centimeters in size, that looked like small little crab, found on white pristine beaches. They inhabited each flowers, waiting motionlessly for their preys. It was eerie but fascinating. Immediately, I began to check my body to ensure that none had crawled on me. Walking through the low shrubs was a challenge and I was constantly checking to ensure none had landed on me. Their form, colours and texture were intriguing, overcame by their quaintness, I summoned all the courage I had and photographed them. They were clumsy too. I believed they were crab spider.

The wild flowers were blooming and colourful. They looked alien, with odd shapes and sizes, some were pungent but attractive. I kept shooting and searched for more subjects. While scouting for more exotic flowers, I was brought to the butterflies. Abundant of them fluttering in shimmering lights reflected from moving leaves and flowers.

I chased the butterflies. They flew, stopped and fluttered away to another flower and another flower. Whenever I got near they started to fly away again.

I was interacting with them and deriving so much fun chasing them. I was also frustrated, disappointed when I could not get as near as I wanted so that they could appear large with magnificent details. I constantly need another better shot and another better shots. The standard zoom lens was all that I had. I did not have a macro lens! The zoom lens that came with the camera was good enough for me to compose the butterfly, the flowers and the leaves all in a single frame, but i was not able to fill the whole view with their portraits alone.

Nevertheless, it was an exhilarating experience.

Returning to Singapore

Upon returned to Singapore, I decided to get a 100mm macro lens, immersed myself for a few months in shooting insects. Why not, I asked myself. I work hard to make some money and I do not spent time to indulge in this passion. Yes, there would be lost in income, no doubt, but time and money not well spend loose its true value too. When we were young, we had time and energy but no money; when we started working we do not have time for ourselves and we had little money but we had a lot of energy; when we had time and money, we found that we lack energy and we are too old to chase our dream. What an irony! What ever I did I had followed my passion and my adventurous calling. Specialization and singularity was not what I had in mind but to lead a diverse life with myriad experiences, however difficult or easy it was going to be, I was ready to accept it. I idolized the Renaissance Man, Michelangelo and Leonado Davinci, men of knowledge, artists, philosophers, inventors, biologists, and city planners. Swapping potential earnings with time for myself was a justifiable proposition. I started my journey into the MicroWorld. I soon realized the immense beauty and wonders of the MicroWorld that I dedicated more time and effort into it without turning back. I had learned so much from the insects and spiders. Inspiration swarmed me everyday as I gazed at them. I was mesmerized; I was absorbed into their amazingly beautiful world. Nature is great!

I started to scout for insects and spiders in Singapore, days were spent at the Botanic Garden and the nature reserve. It seems much simpler shooting butterflies and crab spiders in Inner Mongolia than shooting insects in Singapore. The landscape is a monochromatic dull green and flowerings were sporadic, little clusters here and there, it was never a simultaneous flowering that stretches beyond the horizon. Day lighting was always less warm and more contrastive, resulting in washout details in high light and lack of detail in the shadow. This was acerbated by my inability to get nearer the insects before they flew off, hopped off or crawled off in fright, a defense mechanism that kept them alive. I did some retrospection and soul searching. I realized I was wrong. I was blinded by my desire to see more brilliant colors, exotic forms and stunning actions, that this generated immense anguish and disappointment when they were not fulfilled. I decided to rid my desire to concentrate on the simpler things about life in nature. I began to scan the surrounding at a closer range, got intimate with the plants, the soil and the elements. I soon discovered their abundance wonders. Observing the details on the seemingly insignificant and the minute, I saw their greatness. I was inspired and liberated.

The First Obsession – Proximity

Getting nearer and nearer the subjects became an obsession. There were a lot of common spiders, grasshoppers, dragonflies, and butterflies, but the true obstacle to see them truly as never been seen before was to get nearer such that their sheer enlargement and details become the point of interest, become the triumph and satisfaction, become the enjoyment and inquisition, become immediate knowledge, first hand knowledge, not mediated by others' elaborate textual and pictorial construction, which were contrive and limited by the past. By enlarging the familiar, revealing detail larger than reality, it produces unfamiliarity and interest. A sense of freedom reign within, in quiet observation and reflecting without constraint, learning, interpreting, contemplating, extrapolating, predicting, requesting, guiding, alas in consonance with the subject, in rhythmic pulsation, arriving at the microcosmic world with the subject and its environment. Such immense absorption is liberating and peacefully hypnotic.

With determination, perseverance and practice, slowly I was able to get closer to the subject without alarming them. Sometimes it was a courting process, when they moved, I followed suit, constantly tracking and focusing, persistently trailing, proactively seizing that momentary moment, absorbed and eventually thrilled that I had made that image. I had unknowingly developed the skill and craft to get very close to the subjects, which I was unable to achieve when I started.

The way to getting closer to the insects or spiders is to remove the consciousness of the self. Upon removing the self, the consciousness is directed towards the insects, every nuance would not induce disturbance, as now there is only the insect and itself. Insects are also reacting to our actions, in most instant; theirs are the flight of fright. When the self is non-existence, physicality becomes the environment, quietly observing, and sensing every moves of the insects, consciousness watching and uniting with the macrocosmic world. The camera, has the potential to aid the process of removing the self, like a veil, it helps to hide and dissolve the self. It is a magical instrument, transporting the cameraman towards a selfless consciousness. During the photographing process, the master eyes must affix to the eyepiece of the camera, through this window it transforms, dissolving the identity and the obnoxious self, looking beyond, is the beauty of the Microworld. Never, in a single instant, the eye should leave the eyepiece, or the eye away from the insects, otherwise, the insects may vanish as the consciousness of the self regain itself and the equilibrium is disturbed. The skill of getting closer to the insects needs practices, it is a process that requires transitional space and time. Keep about 30 centimeters between the lens and the subject, keep master eye affix to the camera's eye piece, trigger as you inch slowly toward the insects, your body posture should morph into the environment, creating a firm balance and comfortable position, breathing regulated into a soft diffusing state, ignore your other discomfort, focus, adjusting, moving ever so slowly, left or right, surely nearer, before realizing, the insect is right up next to the lens at the nearest distance possible for obtaining a sharp images at its largest magnification. For a few minutes of such intense concentration, strain and profuse sweating would remind you of fatigue, take it as a regiment for a healthy body and mind. With more practices, the unity becomes a duel of extended slow dance within nature's harmony.

Interestingly, I often sensed that there is a sphere around the insects and spiders I was trying to photographs. Once I have entered this sphere, maneuvering is simpler, it is an indication that the insect have accepted my presence, I would feel honored, grateful and energized. It takes practices and more practices to perfect this process of entering, no amount of reasoning alone can help. It may sound incredible at first, and it will become more incredible once you get a taste of this closeness with insects or spiders. Until this act becomes subconscious and second nature, getting close would be exasperating. Once entered, I would be able to move, though ever so slowly, to compose, frame, and shoot, without inducing the flight of fright. I am receptive and responsive to their every move, as it is a reciprocal situation, each action induce a reaction, moving too close for their comforts may cause them to move away, or sometimes they roved to another location as it was their habits to do so. No ill feeling should be generated if the insects fled, just move on to another insect and another location. They do not sit still as students in classes or workers in factories or professionals in information sweat shops. It is not their nature to do so. They move, change their positions, take chances as often as they would. We are more sedate in urban settings, making the fingers walk rather than the legs. We are domesticated being and we domesticate other animals too. We privilege a sedative life-style – eat, sit and sleep. We mutate to have celluloid filled torso and limbs, then we pay others to mince our flesh so we get to slim down without, again, lifting a finger. Some subject themselves to fat sucking machine or flush their guts to detoxicate. We become dependent, but not the insects' world they are always self dependent; they are responsible for their actions; they have to face the peril of nature, death.

Having the attitude that we are all a part of this Cosmo, indeed a very insignificance part of an infinite universe, we are humbled. I shall respect other beings. I realized that not only the larger animals play their parts, but the smaller animals and invisible forces of nature has a large part to play too. Bees, flies, beetles and ants help to pollinate, break down, and recycle nature and maintain a healthy ecology. Yes, we had been emphasizing the conservation of the four legged animals, birds and fishes such as the White Tiger, the Panda, the Killer Whales, the Dolphins, the Polar Bears, and many others. They were hyped by the Media and we, the urbanites, are led by this global hegemony. We had ignored the larger meaning of life and the forces of nature. Gardens and parks within our reach are ignored, pesticide are rained on the plants to eradicate pests such as mosquitoes or flies, in fact, we had invaded their homes, we love the blooming flowers but not the insects and spiders that were part of this flowering landscape. The residue of the pesticides will settle in the soil or drain into the sea, contaminating the environment and our food chain, eventually poisoning us. It is a slow and revelatory process, its impact may not be immediate, but would definitely be felt by the generation to come. We should reclaim our innocence, our fearless nature, our urge to interact with nature, our being with nature and the universe. We should take a vacation with nature, a journey, albeit an internal one, trace the life of nature, however small or insignificant they may seem, see them take flight, smell their scent, hear their songs and observe our internal changes, mentally and physically. As we settled and associate ourselves with nature, we would also find peace within.

Each meeting with a new insect or spider is the meeting of a stranger. Anxieties, fear, apprehension, shyness, the inability to communicate and interact are the emotion that would run through me. This is normal. My fear and trepidation, were years of prejudice and cultivation that I had acquired, only through a slow process of acquaintance and removal of our inhibition, we could slowly reverse this stigma, receive and feel the abundance of love from nature and the universe. As we visit them more often, better understanding and interaction would take place, we can then get more intimate with them, and the distance between us would reduce. We would understand their habits, characteristics, motion, reactions, features, and live cycles. We knew where to find them, their locations and their season. Their songs are invitations and greetings; we are very much a part of them. From them we established the true meaning of time and space.

The Second Obsession – Rarity

When I first started to look for insects, all I could see was dragonflies and occasionally butterflies. They were so common that I was not motivated to shoot them. I was keener on spotting insects and spiders that I had not seen before. I was impressed by their forms, texture and color. Whenever I found a new insects or spiders, I was elated, I fervently recorded them. I was most impressed by the curvy form of wasps, though they stink, and in some cases cause death to their victims. I had seen primitive wasp, with red oval shape head and glittering purplish thorax with a needle like depositor at the end of her abdomen. It was and still is impressive. Other less threatening insects are the tree hoppers or plant hoppers. They are slow moving though they are well known for their ability to hop; they fly too. They were the earth's best hopper, comparing their height and distance they can hop to the size of the body length. Through the magnifying effects of the macro lenses I could see their amazing forms, their gorgeous saturated colours, and their intricate texture; I saw more than Dali's paranoia dreamscape, it is reality that have been neglected for decades. I fell in love with their forms, texture and color. Though they were available, within our sensory reach, we had not been giving them attention, our focus were on larger animals, or animals in far away places such as the Arctic or Antarctic. Our attention and interest were driven by the main stream media, documentary, books and trends.

As a photographer, a keen one, with the primitive desire to hunt, my camera became the instrument of aggression, I began probing, appropriating, violating, revealing, and transforming the familiar insects into the unfamiliar, jolting and awakening the visual senses of the viewers. This new visual landscape was the motivational force behind each photograph. It is not about understanding them in scientific terms nor objectified documentation, but to instill and build an emotional response, showing them as lively inhabitants of nature, treating them as a part of this universe where we are also a very small insignificant part of it, so insignificant that without us the world would still go on, but without all living things in equilibrium we will not be sustainable. The quest was to bring out the significant in their existence, to turn unfamiliarity into familiarity, fear into understanding, ignorance into acceptance, disgust into appreciation and eventually bring about a wonderful co-existence, and ultimate appreciation of life and discover a world in perfect harmony. The camera, as an alternative eye, has immense power to reveal and change our perception. The camera is a powerful gift.

Learning about Arthropods

I was intrigued by the variety of arthropods. I purchased books on insects, spiders and crustacean. I borrowed books from the library, and spent more time researching on the internet. I soon learned that they have the largest number of species compared to other animals, and they were the least understood. I realized too that entomologists are professionals who study insects. They are a minority profession indeed. I was alarmed to find that due to insects' vast variety, entomologists would only specialize on a particular genus only. They were a constant source of reference when I needed to identify a particular insect. They are extremely helpful and interesting. I began to develop a better understanding of the insects' behavior, life cycles and habitats.

I used social networking site to learn from others, especially the arthropod enthusiasts and the entomologists. From them

I learned about the arthropods' name, special features, habits, behaviors, diet and their evolution. Interacting with them, I develop an intimate and immediate knowing of the insects whose information I garnered from books and the internet cannot help to elucidate, they can only supplement. I soon realized their nuances and the abundant lives that existed within the microcosm of the flowers, leaves, barks, water edges, crevices, rocks, grass, sand, air, on living beings, and other inconceivable spaces.

I learned about biological war being wage against pests using another insects or animals. Phorid flies were cultivated to reduce the population of fire ants in America. American claims that the Fire ants are Asian and they were imported to American through fruits import. Phorid fly lays a single egg on each fire ant, the maggot feed on the host and eventually the host would die a tragic death as it was gutted from inside out. For the ecologically conscious we are glad to learned that ladybirds were sold to garden enthusiasts to combat the growth of aphids, as they can be frozen into hibernation and mailed to the buyers. They are a substitute to the use of environmentally unfriendly pesticide. The abundance of 'Asian Ladybird', once the savior of aphids infested crops, are annoyance to British house owners when they invade their homes and reduce the local Ladybird population, probably due to the decrease in agricultural activities as urban city encroached into the agricultural land, which perhaps have reduced their food supply. The Asian Ladybirds multiply very fast, maps are chartered year after year to plot their invasion of the British Isle. I see these maps with amusement that insects have nationality too.

Sustaining interest

As the days gone by, I would find fewer new insects which I had keen interest to observe and photographs. I was selective. For some days, I did not find any interesting insect; I was not inspired and energized. Then slowly, I begin to experience more and more of these non fruitful day, disappointment started to creep into me and I became less motivated. One fact stuck to me – there are more insects and spiders than any other animals. It was quite impossible to end up in this situation. There must be something which I needed to learn, do, or learn the skill to spot more insects and spiders.

I started to wonder further and further away from where I live. I went to nature reserves such as Bukit Timah Hill, Kent Ridge parks, Changi parks, and Laborador Park. Well, I did found different insects and spiders, but still the numbers remained at one to three insects or spiders found during each visit. Soon I realized whether the parks are near or far do not matter, insects and spiders operate and stay for generations within a few square meters, those that fly have larger operative area, for weeks they can be spotted around the same surrounding. If they disappeared, most probably, some gardeners had spray pesticide in the vicinity, the pesticide that kill Dengue mosquitoes also kills other insects and spiders too, creating an imbalance in the ecological systems and encourages sturdier and creepier critters such as cockroaches, ants and ground crickets. The insect scavengers feed on decomposed bodies. They are usually duller in colors and unattractive.

Since locations do not matter so much, I devised scanning methods to systematically locate insects, I would start scanning from top left to the right, inches by inches, then drop a few inches and again from right to left, repeating it diligently until the grass floor, and then another bush, until I found some insects of interest. This helps to locate most of the insects that reside or operate in that bush. This method allows me to see the relationship between the plants and other living organism, and between the different insects and spiders. I realized that each plant attracts generally the same types of residents or operators. They set up residences and draw up their territory, patrolling, demarcating, setting traps, or cultivating and domesticating other insects for their own purpose and food.

I divided the area to be scanned in 3 distinct areas, those above the eye level, those from the below eye level and those on the ground. Most often, I was scanning at the eye level, as it proofs to be easier on the body, partly because we are animals that stood on both legs and have been doing so for centuries. Scanning the ground needs additional effort and shooting insects that crawl is much more challenging. At times I have to crawl on the floor chasing the ground crickets, the cockroaches, the spiders, beetles and wasps. Insects or spiders on the ground are always on the move, they roamed wildly and they cover wider and larger area as compared to those staying above ground level.

For spiders that build fine horizontal sheet webs, I would prone and shoot at their level. The morning golden sun rays create dramatic dreamscape. Dew droplets glow like diamonds strewn in abundance, lighting the lawn spider in dazzling translucency, as if paradise had descent on the glass blade. The lawn spider would stay watch at the hole in the sheet web, waiting patiently for the right prey to tread on its sheet. The sheet, like a trampoline, vibrates and alert the spider. The sheet does not trap the insect unlike other orb web spun by other spiders. Once it have determined their prey, it would pounce and jab its fangs into the preys, ejecting poison into it and immobilizing it. Under the spell of the poison the prey would collapse and the spider carry the prey away to more secured ground before injecting digestive juice into them and suck in the digested meal.

The least explored are those above the eye level. It is more difficult to reach them with the cameras, unless I climbed on sky-bridge or ladder. In very rare occasion I would find fallen tree which allows me to search for insects at the crown of the tree. I have very few photographs of insects shot high up. I had thought of tree climbing and insect hunting but have yet to acquire the skill to explore this area. I presumed that there will always be differences for insects and spider residing higher up at the crown of the trees and those prowling on the forest floor. I wonder what are those differences. Crawly critters seem to be fatter, darker and have larger barbs at the legs.

While exploring tree barks, I would often find fine spider webs, but not the spider. Once I was so determined to locate the spider, I stood for minutes gazing intensely at the spider webs, still I could not detect any movement. I could not believe this, and I set up the tripods, mounted my macro lens, scanned the area bit by bit systematically, alas I found the culprit. It is the spider perching among the web. However, it was so minute; it was about 1mm in size. That explains the difficulty in locating them.

A few genus of spiders reside on the tree barks, one of them is the white and hairy jumping spider. This jumper prey on small flies about 1mm in size. It loved to do a rapid 180 about turn, checked around, and returned to the original position. Often I could spot golden jumping spider patrolling the yellow flowers and it frequently jerks its celophathorax to a vertical 90 degree. Due to the golden strips on the Celophathorax, there would be flashes and shimmers in the strong sun light.

Awakening - portraits of arthropod

Some days were so uneventful and the challenge becomes the search and find expedition, less of shooting, compositing, creating, and interacting with the insects and spiders. More and more time was spent introspecting and thinking. Then it dawn on me that appreciating and understanding the Microworld is not about finding exotic insects or spiders but capturing their essence, uniqueness and characteristics, however common they are. Through portraiture we could idolized the movie stars, such as Marilyn Monroe, Julia Roberts or Meg Ryan; read into thinkers such as Susan Sontag, Simone de Beauvoir or Ayn Rand; grasped the torment of Pablo Picasso, Georges Braque, Vincent van Gogh, or Marcel Duchamp; understand the differences of time and space; felt the greatness of Mao Zedong, Deng Xiaoping or Vladimir Putin; sympathize with the proletariat, the starving, the underprivileged or the oppressed. Would not portrait of the arthropod well taken and presented could achieve the same impact and bring about a new awakening, a deeper sensitivity and an all encompassing perspective of the world? Presumably it would. The same can be achieved. Is not the Arthropod being marginalized and looked upon as insignificant, whose life could be tempered, trampled, and terminated in a fling of anxiety and slightest of irritation? How could their portraiture charm, gain sympathy and inculcate humanity in us, so that we could be more generous and filled with a deeper sense of humility? Is it a worthy challenge indeed, a mammoth one? Not quite, but it definitely needs time and perseverance.

Photography has the inherent property of being used as a proponent of truth, because its intent was to record and make a copy of reality, albeit limited by the observation and the eye of the photographer, though some photographers are able to capture those details and fleeing moments. The eyes are bound by its ability to differentiate the details that are too minute or too far away or too dynamic. It is still a proof of authenticity and occurrence, unless the photographers go into great length to perfect their art such as the Australian photographer Frank. For Frank, the truth in the photographs was to capture the emotional truth felt during the moment of the despair, triumph, grief, jubilance, and comedy during his expeditions and sojourns to the unknown and uncertainty. He went that extra miles to perfect his skill and art in photomontage, which of course, with the present day application such as Photoshop and Corel Photo would seem easy to achieve. However, the base images were never easy to capture, he risked his life away from his love one to gather those images, and photography with large format, glass plates and movable darkroom, all challenged his determination, endurance, perseverance and faith. He had sheer luck and survival instinct to accomplish so much and brought the unknown world to those who prefer to enjoy those emotion and understanding mediated by his photographs.

Authenticity

There is always a constant debate, within and without, about the authenticity of photograph, any alteration of the image; for some, it is a deadly sin that cannot be pardoned, for others, photography is an art, which has wider and higher objectives, which is malleable, operable, mutable and violable. The accepted norm is that journalistic photography would have to remain truthful, this ethics cannot be violated. However, as an art form, it is left to the parameter set out by the individual artist, he was given free reign to create, even fiction if he wishes. There would be a lot of grey area, if any subject matter is art and yet it is a piece of reality, confusing and convoluting the debate into disarray without a resolution. The portraits of the arthropods would fall into such category, an outsider of sort, recording reality which the eyes had not been able to discern the detail unless mediated by the enlargement of the captured image. They are not scientific proofs for biologists or entomologists; they are imageries that present the micro-reality and a deeper humanly relationship, as his dog would mean to his owner rather than the mice used in experiments conducted by the pharmaceutical researchers. The portraits are more akin to those we made of the famous, the underprivileged, and the unknown. Our revelation is to present their attractiveness, their plight, and their beings. Most general terms are not able to designate and illustrate their peculiarity, leaving us to refer them to their entomological names and classifications, exposing their portraits to further scrutiny by the scientific profession, only constant apologies and clarifications could help in bringing them to the fore, empathizing their beings and their existence as a member of this universe. Their portraits are about them, not whether they belongs to which species, class, order, family, genus, or phylum, these terms constantly haunt us, demanding us to treat them as objects for our investigation and mutiny. This disgusted me. I developed a form of amnesia that helps me to forget and confuse myself wildly, often mistaken one category for another. However, I was please with this confusion and was not willing to conform, prefer instead to concentrate on a direct understanding of them and develop an immediate relationship with them which text and no amount of spoken word would be able to explicate and externalize that awareness. The portraits, thus, had to straddle across, situate between the constraint of the entomological and the primordial knowledge of their beings and existence. Summarily my work assumes a marriage of entomological taxonomy, image and written stream of consciousness, in their contradiction and diversity, perhaps the appreciative spectators would have to decipher and gain insight into the arthropods' world, a little confusion and disparity goes a long way. The photographs are not just about the subjects, but part of me and as much as about the viewers. Their interpretations would reveal themselves, as would the author reveal himself in his work, the text had not been written for the images. The viewers are invited to fill that space. Active participation would make viewing much more enjoyable and fulfilling.

The portraits took the form of realism, less of abstract composition, silently brutal, confrontational, challenges the spectators to scrutinize and in the process discover something. In short, wow them over, made them feel inadequate, humbled, and motivate them to desire more knowledge about the Microworld. Whenever, I showed the photographs to people, sometimes strangers, many were amazed at the form, colour and texture of the subjects. They saw a reality which they had not seen and known. It is inspiring and satisfying for me to see their faces brighten up. It reaffirms my art and the wonders I found in them. However, the image is also a surrogate, a form of mediation with a distancing effect that remove the real subject from the viewer, the viewed is not present in the sphere of the same context as the subject, the viewer is viewing the image in a room devoid of nature, seeing and prying into the photograph through the eye of the photographer, the photographer is the midwife, delivering a certain consciousness and emotion, for remote consumption. Hopefully the photographer midwife would be forgotten and the image takes a life of its own. Who took the iconic image of Marilyn Monroe trying to suppress her uplifting skirts as she stepped over the city sewer? Once consume, it could be addictive and more could be deem necessary to induce more of the same emotion and heavier dosage may be needed to achieve the same effect. It numbed the senses when we were exposed constantly to the same kind of imagery. The freshness turned into staleness, and the image may end in oblivions, forgotten for its novelty, buried deep in some treasure pile as good as wasted trash. Would this superficial quality of form, texture and colour make an eternal impression? Unlikely, you would concord. For the minority few they would have a lasting impact and never get out of it. For the majority viewers, the image has to have other quality that is a constant reminder of something greater, something that have an intrinsic value, something that touches their heart every time they glance at it. Soon I found the thrill and satisfaction of discovering weirder insects and spider wares off. I was back to where I had started, not having that unstoppable need to discover and shoot. The aspiration of wanting to discover a new visual elements and share with others, seems as unlikely to fascinate the viewer for too long as I was not convince myself.

The Surrogate

The photographer, the surrogate mother, feels the entire process, the context surrounding the circumstances when the photograph was made. She feels the happiness, the discomfort, pleasure, weight, agony and the being within her.

She would develop hormone, anxiety and tiredness. She would change physically, enter another physiological stage and psychological state of mind; she made adjustments to all these changes. She knows that the baby, of other's genes and composition, when delivered, belongs to another world, and not hers to keep. She knows her labour of several months will come to pass; her process will come to an end upon that moment of delivery and birth. Good photographs are labours of pain and happiness. The photographer is the loner in this journey; she carries the weigh, joy or pain, no amount of psychological support can sooth or take away that physical and psychological demand. She is the bearer, the sole bearer. Only she understood the context which existed within her. It is an individual journey, where the fruition, would take a life of its own, and becomes communicable. However, some photographers may fall into depression, as the pain and grief of the process stayed with them, their inability to escape those agonizing moment led them to end their lives. The more their images were appreciated by the public, the more burdens they felt, the more guilt they acquired, not because of the inability to help, but the fame and mileage they garnered from others miseries, made them an anti-hero, defying the trust of the weak had bestowed on her, a traitor within them. Inside them, the traitor must be punished and pay for their crime. They become their subjects and subsume by their inescapable destiny; they were traumatized. Death then becomes the exit. Diane Arbus, famous for her work on people with abnormalities, ended her life. Another war photographer ended his. A Photographer of Africa. Others challenge those circumstances and took up the responsibility to make changes so that their grief can be redeemed and their conscience cleaned. They are the activist photographer. The Brazilian Photographer, honored by Berkely.

The same miseries existed in any living beings, so too are the arthropods. No life can escape miseries, such as disease, inadequacy, imperfection, pain, and ultimately death. However, the possibility of miseries of the arthropods having an adverse effect on the photographers or observers is inconceivable, as I seldom heard of anyone championing their plight as their sizes are so negligible and therefore their lives are so insignificant that any human who would sacrifices his life for them seems absurd. I had not heard of anyone scarifying his life for the arthropods. Such pessimistic hazard is non-existence. There is no model release to sign or model fee to be paid. No complicated law suit by people claiming for compensation after being featured in publication. The peril of dealings with images of human subjects is, sometimes, tedious, unpredictable; it could ruin one's creative endeavor and diminished his drive. Such freedom and creative possibility existed in nature photography. Landscape, flowers, plants and animals, they do not demand after the image was made. If there is any demand, they were being made during the shooting process, and never there after. The peril was being bitten by them knowingly or unknowingly. However, precautions and preventions can be taken and most often very effectively circumventing those consequences.

Fear and nature

I could find the same worldly miseries in the Microworld, famine, wars, flood, deformity, destructions, birth and death. Although they are minute, it too happens. It is a Microcosm of the Macrocosmic world that we had been experiencing. Initially there was that ambiguity, the insect hunting drive, a sadistic male instinct, when faced off with the cannibalistic death of the weak and susceptible, I struggled to resolve the sense of inability of the self and my inadequacy.

I fear insects and spiders, as would any other normal being, though I shoot them at close range. Many were surprised by my confession and weakness, assuming that I am a lover of insects and spiders, therefore logically I would be fond of them and unafraid of them. It is otherwise. My love for them is the quest for a peek into their mysteries and wonders; they never fail to astonish and awe me, but I am not attracted to them like bees to honey. The relationship is remote. I appreciates them from a distance. That distance was afforded by the closeness between the lens and camera. The closest of which is when I try to achieve a hundred percent magnification. The lens and camera is the shield and the gap between me and the insects. The separation forms part of the reason for me to be a keen observer and non-activist.

When faced with their miseries, the internal struggle was whether to interfere with nature's cruelty or ignore them. I reasoned, what I perceived is the flow of nature. It is what nature is all about. The sustainability of life is a circular complex web, nature are forces that transform from one to another. Take for example the ecological food chain, one animal or plant is food for another animal, and it is in turn the food for other animal. No amount of intervention can change this law of nature. What I need to change and subdue is the emotional eddy of morality. I need to remain resolve and calm. I adopt the position of inaction, though I am so gigantic and powerful compared to the insects and spiders, I am actually powerless faced with the being of nature, I felt diminished and insignificant. I felt small and vulnerable. So my weak and humble self could escape the altruistic responsibility and burden to avoid committing the crime of nature. Martyr or villain is a narrow line, the same can be said of genius and a mad man. Socrates' unceasing mode of questioning is at once the poison and cure for the mind of the youth and intelligent soul. Drug is both a poison and a cure. Socrates drank hemlock to proof his innocence and allayed the fear of the authority whose form of reality cannot be shaken. Such unshaken conviction and courage. We admire him, chastise his virtue. But few of us would emulate him. I do not have the courage and innocence so great. I am just a diminutive individual dangling a fake 'gun' pretending to hunt, enjoying the adrenalin rush when each trigger was release; it seems perverse. Yes, it is an urbanite perversion. I let nature takes its course. I found peace and reasonable humanity within. My inaction would seems harsh, cold and mysterious, as I took the form of nature, action is regarded as an intrusion, invasion and mutilation of the great art of nature. I only see the thing itself as they appear and unfold before me. I am an observer, aware of the happenings, unaffected. I felt silence and calm. I found solitude in inaction. The truth in my art is its exactitude and precision, framing them as I see them from my perspective and limitation. I am the documenter of the fleeing moment of intangibility, a savior of light, a conservative, a treasure seeker, that conjure things from evanesce. In a way, I create, like a magician, conjuring reality and making them tangible and real, as commodity for consumption and appreciation. The viewers are experiencing nature further behind the second layer. I am the in between, that liberates and limits their experience, and constraining it into some potent visual frames. They, the viewers, consume gleefully.

The viewers are behind the photographer; they only see. They are removed of other sensory experience, such as auditory, olfactory, touch and kinestatic. They posture in standing or sitting position while reviewing the images at arm length. The context was displaced, the gap was unfulfilled, stripping the discomfort and ugliness, the arthropods images seems more palatable in a clean and luxurious display room. The visual silence overpower its limitation, demanding the viewers to fill in the gap, which may fluctuate according to their emotional state, but persuaded by the brilliance of nature's colors and optimism, play out soothing melody, romanticizing the circumstances, deriving immense pleasure and joy. Nature always has the power to cure and redeem the troubled soul. The image of natures, including those of arthropods, would be a good substitute where nature is remote in the urban setting, immersion in these imageries could perhaps be a pseudo cure. Such is the potency of brilliantly colored and well photographed arthropods. Who would prefer the insectariums, the insect crematorium, where the dead of the Microworld are exhibited and admired for their rarity, placid form, faded color and crinkled texture? What brilliance could be well preserved in the dead, except diminished glory. How much brilliance can death contained, but a dull lifeless pastiche. Tourists with happy faces would not mind visiting them, but not the war memorial or their dead heroes in the mausoleum. The camera is one of the few instruments that can capture the fleeing happiness, grief and struggle, making them eternal and gratifying the viewers at their command. All these are, but the illusion of the urbanite, me and you alike. We love a good narrative and a good emotional trip. It makes us feel alive.

2. Attitude

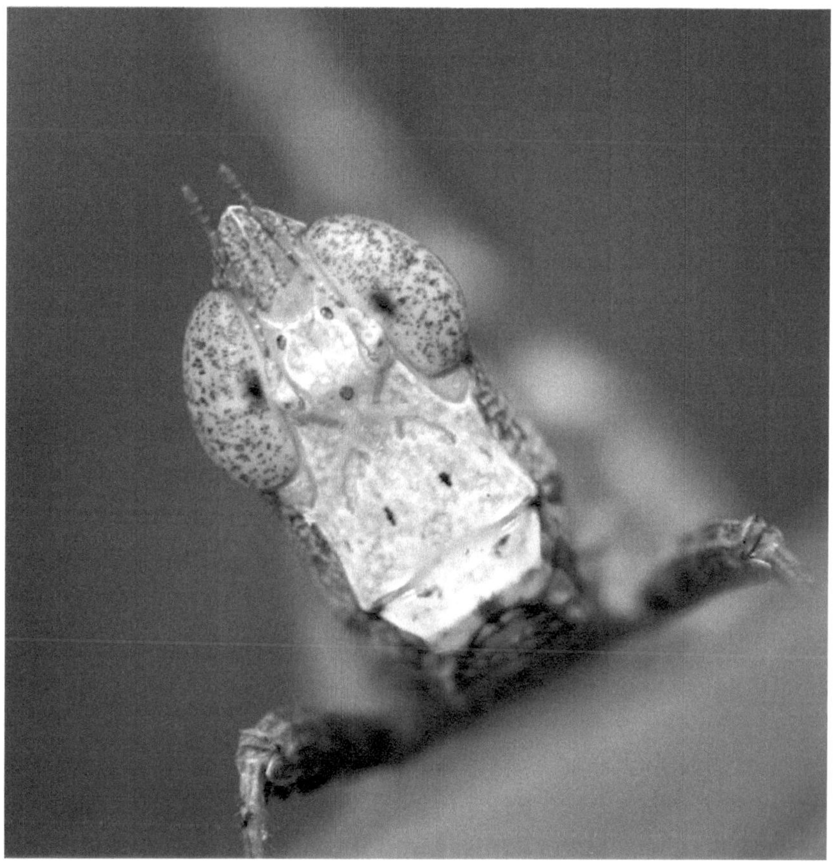

From observing nature and arthropods, I have learned and gained invaluable insight into their world and our world. Their juxtaposition, make me see our similarities and differences. In fact, we are all family members of this wonderful world of lives. The amazing energy of life exists simultaneously in things big and small, as minuscule as any microscopic device can magnify or as far as the telescope could reach. Though the scientific calculation of time with the tickling clock put a discrete denominator for all living things' length of existence, it could not escape the circumstances of birth, life and death. It is the eternal truth. The 'in betweens' are just variations and possibilities, there were no right or wrong. One form of life's termination is the continuum of another, without which the other ends. None has commit crime that ought to be punished because of their murderous traits. Life is cruelty and beauty.

We too are carnivorous except the vegetarians; we eat other animals, including insects and spiders. When I first thought of eating insects, I felt disgusted and disgusting. I got the first taste when visiting Linyi, a city about 600 kilometers north of Shanghai, China. I was presented with their local delicacy – pan fried Cicada nymph. They looked so harmless and my host was savoring them with great contentment. They urged me to try it and with a lot of courage I took my first bite. It was soft and less scary than I had imagined, but not as delicious as my host had conveyed. The most scary bit was the Cicada faces, very alien looking when view directly. It still haunts me until today.

Should people eat insects? And why not? Are people a lesser being and uncivilized eating insects? Some may hold this view, but others never considered it that way. It is a tradition for some tribes and urban dwellers to eat insects and spiders. They had such practises for centuries. Perhaps it is a practice derived from famine and drought, or traditional believe of their potency and aphrodisiac effects that has legitimized the custom. Every seemingly absurd practice or normal practice would require reasons to establish their existence, otherwise, when this demand is ignored, it would be deem superstitious and has to be abolished accordingly, a rational modern society seek truth and answer for everything. We seek incessantly for answer in everything and every being. Is the unceasing quest, a necessity for our being and our existence?

Do we need to know who we are or our purpose of living, in order to have a reason to appease ourselves that we are on the right path and our existence is legitimate? Is that consciousness attainable? Ever? Or should we experience every detail, nuance and moment of this moment? As those who seek will find the answer, so should not we just experience the moment? Which is more real? Which is more truthful? We arrive at the basic question of what is life. Or what is the life worth living.

Perhaps we can find some answer from nature. Observing nature and the little critters. We see the repetition of the critters' life cycle. We saw our repetition too. Don't we love variation, and privilege novelty? We do. When did we start to privilege novelty and disregard repetition as a virtue? Why don't we love repetition? Most of us, unlike the existentialists that found nothingness in life, yearn and demand a meaningful life that has the highest value and eternity, we disbelieve a transient existence that end in absurd insignificance, like the seemingly valueless life of the ants and bees, whose reason for existence is not an end in itself, they serves others, being nature. We would never accept that conclusion.

Albert Camus found salvation in the struggle, the process is all that is to life, his analogy in the The Myth of Sisyphus, where the recurring effort in pushing the rock up the hill to see it rolls down after reaching the peak and push it up again to roll it down again. This process repeats eternally. At first glance, it seems a destiny of achieving nothing, no high aim, no salvation, just recurrence and eventual boredom. However, if we recall those moments in our lives which we were proud and happy, often we are most impressed by those in which we had overcome adversity and live through its irony. We would recall in light-heartedness, remembering tough times, however we would not hesitate to do it again given another chance. The struggle and triumph become the worthiness and meaning of existence. Experience is all that is to life and our existence, in order to reign freely across all experiential landscape, we may trespass the boundary of morality . Backpacking and traveling is one such activity that grew out of existentialism. Of course the theatre of the absurd (*Théâtre de l'Absurde)*, a term coined by Martin Esslin pushed that borders even further. We will see all these absurdities in the Microworld, which appear absurd because it is alien to us, a discordance with our lives and we have not spend time experiencing the microworld.

The mosquito's life may not last more than a season so the mosquito born in summer will never know the coldness of winters. Cicada spend all their life burrowing underground, surfacing only to mate and die within a month or less. Some Cicada, the Periodical Cicada, could spend as much as 17 years underground without seeing daylight, their lives may seem miserable to us, perhaps they could be having great fun burrowing. Many spiderlings will not survive till maturity and be independent, hunt and provide for themselves. From observing the Microworld, as detail as the eyes can discern, I could see the same recurrence that repeating many times within human's life cycle of 70 years. I saw their transiency. For those that out live us, I sense their eternity.

Observing the Microworld, we see the inexplicable universe. I constantly found strange colours, shapes and textures in Microworld. Their behaviors and motions, when scrutinized never resemble those of human being and the four legged animal. Their residences and habitats are even more bizarre, outlandish and never would appear in the canvass of the surrealists, surmounting those by Salvador Dali that were produced with the Paranoiac-critical method. One great difference is that though they contain the quality of the absurd, they are, in fact, real and existed among us for a long time; we have neglected their existence and we continue to do so. Now, is the moment to reclaim that bewilderment, wonder and uncertainty to reaffirm this microworldly existence. The world, is, but the theatre of the absurd, if we scrutinized them in detail. Our inability to phantom this world and our existential condition, provided our acceptance of an Artuadian description or resignation.

Immersing constantly in an Microworld long enough, I gain familiarity and the materiality of reality, I began to see that existence is a simultaneous consistency of this absurdity. I became the absurd and accept this monotony and homogeneity. They are the banal and profane. Slowly the recurrence, form a genius loci in my memory, as I experienced the sense of rootedness in this surrounding that I have circumscribed, touched, watched, fantasized, enjoyed and participated. My existence and their existences are knitted into a tight inseparable oneness. This oneness is experienced in a momentary bliss, as in bliss, it has the quality of temporality with a great sense of fulfillment; it is not lasting. It flips often to the mundane, the artificial and the superficial. From this banality, again I begin to map colors, meaning and emotion on them, experiencing and feeling fulfilled. It is necessary for us to grasp our existence and acquire a sense of place, situating ourselves in relation to the world. Fluctuating between coloration and indifference to see the unity, the meaningful and the meaningless situation, I experience the wonder of life. We ought to love recurrences; it is a form of ritual. We love these rites and it is Art. The moment we infuse art into the recurrence of nature, we fuse beauty with repetition, we perfect the rite and make each experience wondrously beautiful. Existence become full when life is Art; art is everything in nature. Hence, only an aesthetic life is worth living – the only salvation.

As people congregate in the city, the amount of green and nature which we could experience have shrunk tremendously. For a well planned city, about 35% of the land is retained as green. They are either designed as pockets of garden or larger nature reserve that conserves flora and fauna, including smaller animal such as insects and spiders. They are proofs of our existence and a fragment of reality which can be traced and understood in Darwinian Theory of Evolution. Thus a lineage and connection is made, that we are derived from the simplest life form and evolved to the present complexity and naivety. We bring nature, albeit superficially without exposing ourselves to its bareness and rawness, into gardens and parks, so that we can at once be with nature and the universe, while residing within the comfort of the artificiality of urban setting. We strip nature, retain those friendly elements, remove pests and unsightly living organism, deploy and arrange aesthetically pleasing materials, soothing our ego and soul. We purified, designed, selected, and moulded nature, negating and suppressing other menacing life form that threaten our chances of survival; we want safety and the virtue of both world, nature and urbanity.

It is a plausible idea. Highly urbanised cities and countries evolved from the Agrarian Society, struggled through the macabre Industrial Age and entered the Information Society. This age arrives at the flood gate of information overload, democratizing of the media, speeding up of connection and networking, flattening of time and space, creating multiple possibility of existence, demanding greater adaptability and malleability from one culture, one climatic condition, one geography, to another, answering to the differences in time and space. We have a lot to grapple with, balance, and calm ourselves to face all these myriad choices and multiplicities. We parallel process, gaining ability of the computer chips, fervently consuming, digesting, assimilating, churning out, creating, eking out a decent living and realizing a new world order. We are drained most of the time. We are tired. We have to return to nature. Learning from the Microworld and nature is the salvation, the return, the reconciliation with an aesthetic life.

3. Sex

While in the park if we scrutinize nature closely, chances are we would see insects flying, crawling, hanging, or courting. We would also see beetles, flies, butterflies and dragonflies in their procreation act. Sex is the magical process of fusion between two different sexes of the same species, out of which, something happens, something is given power to live, to grow and come into being. All nature's continuity depends on the process of procreation. In nature, myriad of lives are created constantly. We celebrate birth and associate it with fortune. We are refreshed and are full of hope whenever we immerse ourselves in nature's embrace. When we are sick or depressed, we believe we can recharge, clear our minds and recuperate in a natural environment. Nature has the property to cleanse us of all urban ills. Nature is beautiful and wonderful. Truly, magical!

All living things propagate in diverse and creative ways. Whenever I saw their procreation process, I am thrilled and startled. I have immense respect for the greatness of nature and the varieties of the process, though it was a simple act of fusion. Bees, flies and beetles are more than match makers for plants; they are the medium for fertilization. Their responsibility is mammoth and tedious. Imaging if human is the medium, we would hate that repetitive act and we probably would not be able to complete the task, given the amount of plants that require the service. I am grateful to them. Whenever I drink fruit juice, I am glad and thankful. I savor it fully, treasuring their efforts.

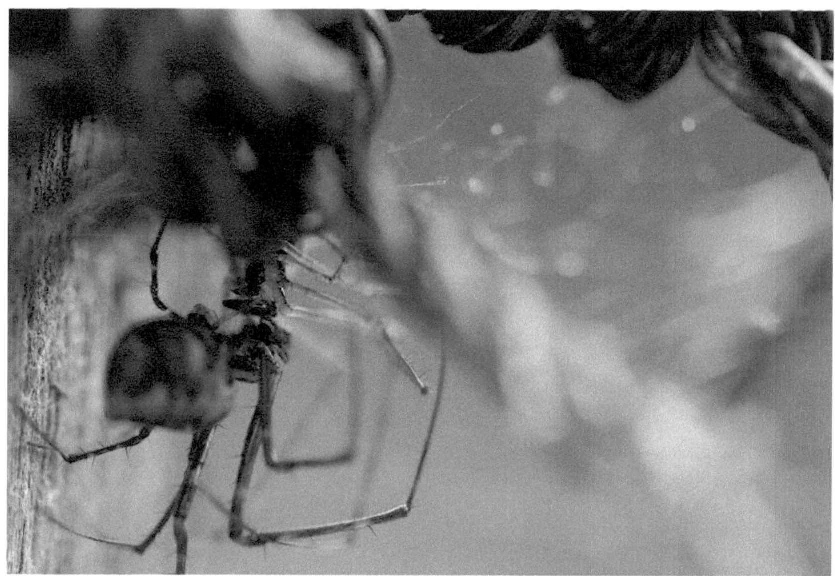

It is extraordinary to see spiders mating and even when we saw them mating, we may not be aware that they are mating, because their procreation positions are ambiguous and obscure. In fact, books had been written on spider Karma Sutra, it spell out and illustrate the various sexual positions adopted by spiders. For those who love sex, perhaps you can possibly learn a thing or two from the spiders. One such position is known as the Spider Web. When it comes to sex, they are the sexiest, erotic, kinky and playful of the small animals; some of their acts can last hours.

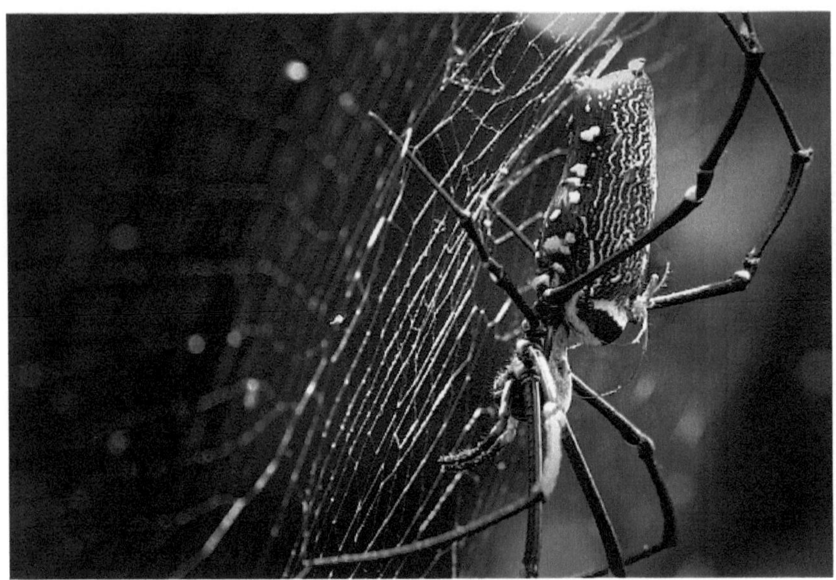

One such ritual was performed by the minuscule male Nephila Malacuta. The male spider is only about one tenth of the size of the female Nephila Malacuta. He has to be very cautious when approaching and mating the female, less he may be eaten up.

Spider has a pair of male reproductive instrument, known as the palps which produce sperms and ejaculate them into the Epigyne of the female spider. The palps are located beside the fangs, near the mouth. Sex becomes a little awkward and requires some ingenuity and creativity. Swollen palps indicate a male spider.

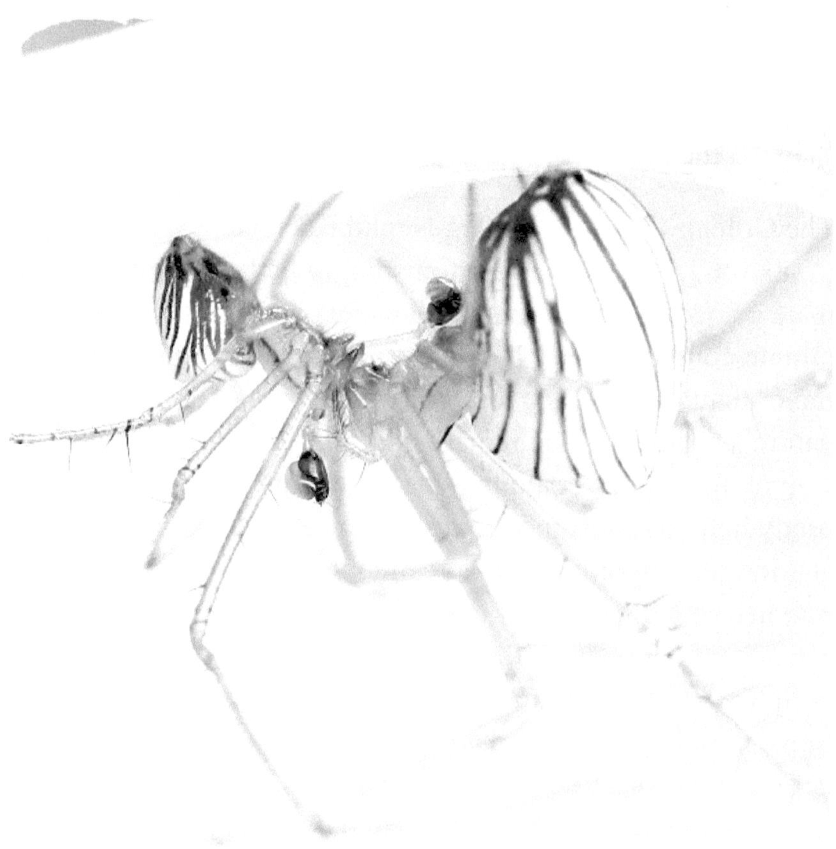

I am particular impressed by the Linyx Spider's palps. It is red with transparency and shape like two blobs embracing each other terminating in a needle, for ejaculation I presume. The female spider's reproductive organ is known as epigyne, usually a curvy slit on her underside, whereas some may get very complex.

Male spider has to prepare before courtship, by soaking up sperms from the abdomen into the palps. He first make silk web and squirt some sperms into it and then suck it up using the palps. Courtship itself can take hours. He dances around the female and vibrates his front limbs, waves his palps and release pheromone to attracts and subdue the female. Once the female is ready and signal readiness, the male spider would then approach her, adopt the sexual position and inserts the palp into her epigyne, each palp would take turn to insert the sperms.

The Golden Orb Web Spider, Nephila Maculata was known to sex for 15 hours. More astonishingly is the size of the male compared to the female Maculata. The male is so minute comparatively; it can be mistaken to be spiderling rather than the husband, only one tenth of the female's size – nature's absurdity. The female built the strongest and largest web of all spiders, spanning one to two metres. The male is pretty helpless, designed to depend on the female for food and lodging, upon maturity, abandoning his web and move into her web through self invitation. He spent times to romance the female spider, he would dance for hours at the peripheral of the web, tapping the silk web rhythmically, and move in only when he is sure that she is ready or she just had her meal. He has to be careful, otherwise, very easily, he becomes the diet of the female. He mounts her usually on the dorsal first and moves to the underneath to copulate with her. Due to the great difference in size, he has no choice but to adopt the missionary position. Upon accomplishing his mission, he has to retreat carefully behind her. She is never short of male in waiting, on average she will have 2-3 male partners who have to risk their life, all depending on their skill and her generosity, to survive the process of planting their seeds to propagate the next generation. This is worst than rejection during teenagers' courtship, as they are a matter of death and birth. Some competition was so keen that the female could have eight males in waiting. She digs a hole on the ground, spins some silk web in the hole, lays the eggs and then covers them up with soil or rot.

4. The Insecthunter

The Swordsman

For a few thousand years, the sword had been the weapon of choice and swordsmanship is a form of worship. The warrior symbolizes the supreme mind and life, not many human being could reach the pinnacle of attainment. He dances in perfection with the least movement and precision to bring down his evil opponents. He is attuned with his environment. When he observes he is as still as the rock and when he strikes he is as swift as the hawk. He strikes effortlessly with ease. Simplicity is the highest form of his Art. This art is beauty and life. Life is Art. Art is living. Art is everything there is in this universe. His teacher would see to it that he practises his art from a young age. He is trained to be one with his sword, his art and his environment. The sword is the symbol and reminder of his art and his only guardian of his art, justice, righteousness, patriotism, loyalty, love, compassion, knowledge, self-discipline, control, faith, believe and path to perfection. He makes a pact with his sword that when the sword is drawn, as it is sacred, only when necessary, it is a ritual, there is only beauty and the sword only return when it has tasted some blood. Oneness is that perfect moment when he, the sword and the universe is one, he sees only his opponent and how they would fall. It is a fleeing moment which comes and reached the end in one continuous stroke and dance. It started in stillness and ends with stillness. Bliss and death is a single continuum. His art is his truthful expression and he never betrays his sword. With his sword, he never needs to betray himself; he has the power to be honest. He does not need to bow to evil, greed, and desire. He would avoid them and retreat to his sanction away from their corruption. However when they demand his attention and he has no place to escape, he would face them bravely, ending this feud in a dance of Art, death and sacrifice. He is always truthful to his sword and his life is his sword. He is willing to die for his sword and an honest self expression. It is an honorable death. It is an aesthetic life that is worth living! The spirit of the swordsman is so appealing, but unattainable in this information society where urban order and condition is palatably comfortable. Education and family life is the pinnacle sought by all urban dwellers. There is hardly any worshipper of the spirituality of the swordsman. But there are always some exceptions, as the curse of the sword calls them into their existence, complete their life in this sacrifice for art. Yukio Mishima is one such exception, committed to the way of the Samurai.

The Sniper

The gun was invented after the European improved the quality of the gun power from the Chinese. From Chinese's fire canon ball launched from the bamboo tube to the canon of the west, the same principal is used in the gun. The first gun, the Matchlock was developed around 1400s. Gradually, the sword was substituted by the canon and the gun in warfare, as it is easy to operate and they kill from a distance. The pistol was the way to settle personal feud, defend justice and individual right. A weak individual with the skill to aim and squeeze the trigger could kill another from a distance, acquiring immense power with little training and self discipline. This is the attractiveness of the rifle and pistol. Deadly power come within one's reach regardless of his physical prowess. Canons and guns are the instruments of coercion employed to colonize other countries. The popularity of the sword dwindled but the spirit of swordsmanship, honor and loyalty could not be replaced. The sword of honor remains the most sought after status in the army. Officers during peace time, dress with the sword hanging by his side. The spirit of the swordsman resume its magical power in the sniper, of stealth and endurance, of dedication and honor, of loneliness and sacrifice, bestow with faith and discipline, his individual strength could accomplish much more than that of many, changing the outcome of wars and politics. The sniper is the modern swordsman. It assume the quality of art, discipline and honor, differentiating infantry soldiers from the highest form of soldiering and shooting, which many soldier sought to attain. This honor is only reserved for the privilege of being a member of the prestigious unit, the sniper unit.

The Camera

Everyone wears a camera or a mobile photo with a camera, the modern substitute for the sword or the rifle is the camera. Camera shoot! There is no actual death or sacrifices, but a metaphorical death of the moment, where the moment had passed and was immortalized on digital camera. Camera kills time. It is death and liberation. The moment is gone but it's spirituality is imprinted on film, making permanent the slice of evidence, the essence and spirit lives forever as it can be recalled, shared and re-lived in the mind of the viewers, whose presence transverse the limits of time and space. The camera replaces the responsibility of the sword and rifle. Placing the power in the hand of the individual, whose revelation of the imagery could help to raise sensibility and passively persuade changes. Instantaneously it would reach the world when posted on the web or email, circulating the globe and liberating the mind of the viewers. Emotion would fly and knowledge is obtained through myriad interpretations colored by their differences in cultures and believes. Without all these biases, prejudices and privileging of one form or another, these images are slices of meaningless happenings. Reading is derived and the image is consumed, satisfying the primordial need for heroism, fulfilling the societal need of making and worshipping of the hero. Vietnam War, its atrocities, committed by Americans and Vietnamese, left indelible marks on American citizens, Nick Ut's photograph of a nine-year-old girl running toward the camera, fleeing a South Vietnamese napalm attack, together with other vietnam war photographs, succeeded in waking up the sensibilities of the world, averting a prolong war in Vietnam. The photographer is the modern days' hero. He champions the weak and the underprivileged.

The Insecthunter – the last frontier

Many photographers armed themselves with cameras, hunt down and immortalize events, peoples and animals. Their greatness was to risk their live or spend their entire life bringing great moments within our reach so that we can sensitize ourselves in our urban comfort. So that we could momentarily feel their agony, sorrow, excitement, happiness, grief or anger through their photographs. Their works are reflections of their attitudes, characters and their subjects. They are not just hunters; they are devoted hunters. Many animals had been hunted, especially the vertebrates, avid photographers armed with long lenses stake out in Africa safari hunt down lions, tigers, leopards, cheetahs, buffalos, deers, wolfs, dogs or any four legged animals that crawl. They dived deep into the sea to hunt for the whales, dolphins, stingrays, gigantic jelly fishes, and providing us visual entertainment, enriching our senses and experience. The least photographed, are the arthropods, they have the largest number of species on earth, except they are tiny compared to vertebrates. Smallness makes them insignificant, neglected up till now. We are conscious of their existence only when we start to frame and enlarge their world with macro cameras. We begin to take notice and are attracted to their world, seeing them up close for the first time, consumed by their beauty and magic, we took up arm and become the insecthunters. There are Africa safari, night safari, bird park, underwater world and insectariums. We should have microworld safari to explore the last frontier of the animal kingdom, to assume and reclaim the hunter in us, uniting our being and art within.

Holding the camera in the hand, the psychic took on the persona of the hunter, awareness was heighten, each release of the shutter was a good shot being fired, nailing the image that was anticipated. Yes, anticipated. The actual shot is never the image that was seen before a sudden black out because there was always a lag from the instant when the eye saw and the mind decided, the mind then alerted the neuron to pass instruction to the finger, the finger started to depress the shutter, the shutter release travelled a few millimeter downward to trigger, the mirror flipped up, the aperture constricted and the shutter curtain opened to register the image, the image temporary burned the sensors, electronic pulses was converted into digital algorithm residing in the random access memory and then written into the solid state memory. So much complexity in the process, although it is so simple to make a single picture, but a lot practises are required to acquire the skill of precision in delivering the shot. Anticipation that matches the shot in the mind eye acquires experience and intense observation. Observation helps to predict and replay the action. All living things are in constant motion. Motion is relative, the camera moves, the environment moves and the object moves; the resulting image is different, requiring anticipation to achieve the composition and expression. The sniper understands this perfectly in order to hit the target at the correct spot. When the finger depressed the trigger, the bullet leaves the barrel, travels for sometime before it reaches the target. It could take seconds if the distance is two kilometer away. In that few seconds, the target could have move away from the targeted point. Understanding the subject, in this case the behaviour of the particular arthropod is crucial in predicting their motion and action.

Life is Art

The swordsman is an artist. The sniper is an artist. The insecthunter is an artist. The sword is a piece of art. The rifle is a piece of art. The camera is a piece of art. Leica is a piece of art, the *otaku* photographer, the collector collect them to own a piece of art. The shine of the multicoat, the design, the simplicity, the palm size, the silent trigger, the non-descript form and humility transformed us into connoisseur of form and beauty. However, aesthetic appreciation of the camera and lens, is not enough to summon the artist in us, we need to hunt, shoot, perfect the moment, dance with nature, unite and be one. Practise, more practices and intense concentration would bring out the artist in us. Ultimately, the Insecthunter as an artist.

A sniper will have to understand his weapon precisely, in order that the bullet hit the target with one shot and one kill. Other soldiers, especially those with the general purpose machine gun would think otherwise. Most would think that since there is so many shots fired, at least one shot would get the target, and that would eliminate the target. Similarly, a lot of camera handlers adopt the same believe, setting the continuous firing mode and fire away so that by chance one image would turn out great. Camera maker would make such claim that a fool could have the potential to shoot a master piece. If a million images are made, therein would contain that single image that is as great as the art of Davinci or Michelangelo. Master piece became a number game of randomness and erroneous pursuit. However, a sniper, a worthy photographer, believes in the art of handling weapon, the achievement is that one single shot, one single image, one piece of art. The intended result is achieved with the least effort and material. It is the art and beauty of simplicity that attracts the aspired who love the challenge. Simplicity is simple to achieve once all complex details are managed, considered, calculated and executed with a single effective stroke.

Zeroing

All weapons have to be zeroed. The rifle's zeroing is done with a fixed range, this account for peculiarity of the eye, the placement of the cheek on the butt, the finger squeezing biases. Each time the position and the squeezing pressure should not change, each squeeze moves the weapon slightly, affecting the flight path of the bullet. The weight of the weapon and the size of the round decide the maximum range of the weapon that could reach the target. The M16 has the maximum range of about four hundred meters, the General Purpose Machine gun can reach one thousand five hundred meters and the M2 BMG could be lethal at a range of two kilometres. Carlos Hathcock established the record of a kill at 2,286 meters. Special viewing device and scope is required to see the target. The camera needs zeroing too. Ansel Adams employed the zone system to zero his camera and the film. It is a laborious trial system, which ensure maximum tonal range, which takes into account the effect of chemical processing, the method of processing, the peculiarity of the films and the setting of the camera, especially its film speed, i.e. ISO or ASA speed. The digital camera needs zeroing too, test shot with colour chart and multiple electronic setting need to be set to the preference of the photographer. Each camera is pre-tune to the liking of the photographer, so that he sees the result he envisions.

Every image is a precise execution. The scene must first be seen, framed and composed. Lighting condition is evaluated and camera setting such as ISO, shutter speed and aperture is selected before releasing the shutter to eternalize the moment. ISO determine the sensitivity of the film or light sensor, its variation has impact on the final image, images are noisy at higher ISO. Colour are also less rich and saturated, shadow area has less detail and could be dirty brownish patches. Each camera's senor performs differently. In fact, ISO could reach 100k that it is now possible to shoot in moonlight, offering another visual landscape that is not possible previously. Night hunting is another possible activity. For an image not to show blurriness or movement, the camera or the subject needs to be still. Movement is the relativity between image movements on the film or sensor plane and the amount of detail, determine by pixel length in digital or film sensitivity that can be captured by the camera. A vertical or horizontal movement across the camera plane registers more changes as opposed to a movement approaching or diminishing away from the camera perpendicularly. However, in reality, most movement are at acute angle to the camera, making estimation of which shutter speed to adopt for a particular situation tricky. The aperture, determine the depth of field, define as the distance within which the image remains acceptably sharp. It has the most impact on the pictorial landscape of the image.

The Mass adoption of the camera as a necessary individual productivity tool has pushed camera technology to the level where the digital has over taken the film camera. However, insect hunting is not about owning a piece of technology, but about having acquire a way of seeing and presenting the view point of the hunter. The hunter needs to be familiar with his camera as he continues to engage the insects or spiders, while his fingers adjust the exposure, the aperture, the shutter speed, the ISO, white balance and lighting compensation. The master piece is made only when all these variables are precisely executed.

Understanding the characteristic of light and shadow, and selecting the right angle are crucial. As the camera move from left to right, reflection and highlight is constantly changing, the subject's posture, shape, size and color rendering changes too. Daylight changes as it has to pass through the atmosphere which is mediated by the clouds, wind and air density. Daylight is such an illusive medium that changes every second, color varies as the intensity of light striking the subject changes, frequently compounded by reflected light that bounces off other surfaces bringing with it the tint of the surface, light diffracts through the air, glass, plastic or water diffuse onto the subject surfaces. All these, determine that every second the image has no duplication and the resulting image cannot be duplicated in an existing light situation unless it is artificially set up in a controlled studio environment. Shooting a picture requires the coming together of the accidental and perfecting the predictability of the image; it is an art rather than science.

Each lens is built for a different purpose. For shooting the Microworld, it would be necessary that a macro lens is used or a point and shoot camera with a macro function. Each camera and lens has its peculiarity, and they perform optimally at a particular setting. Each lens has a focusing distance where the image is sharpest. A certain size of the aperture will give the best sharpness and it is not always that smaller aperture means sharper picture. The manufacturer will provide a general test report that shows how the lens will perform and which would affect the captured image.

Spotter and the insect hound

In fact, snipers work in pair, one shoots and the other spots. Similarly, any hunting game with weapon, or camera with huge magnification makes locating the target very demanding, especially when the target is ducking around and moving in an irregular manner. Camera with macro lens or long telephoto lens has the same limitation and faces the same problem. In arthropod hunting, having a spotter, preferably an entomologist, otherwise anyone who is willing to accompany him would suffice or when alone, the trick is to alternate the left eye and the right eye, one see normally and the other see the magnified image. Most often it is a lonely hunting game. Few people would have the patient watching and waiting for that one shot that took many hours of waiting and observation. Many would prefer the sound of machine gun firing and the visual of splattering material, driving the audience's adrenaline up keeping their heart pounding. Arthropod hunting is uneventful, too much preparation for too little action. There is no such drama. Perseverance and immense patient are required to track and move into position before the actual action. Little was mentioned about the effort put in by the sniper to close in for the kill. Movies always emphasized and dramatized the tense moment when the trigger was pulled and the circumstances surrounding the subjects. However, the challenge is getting near without alarming the subject, while the danger is lurking in the unknown. We call the photographer hunting images of the arthropods the Insecthunter; he too moves in the danger of being bitten by snakes, wasps, bugs and mosquitoes.

The Air and movement

The density of the air and the movement of the air, wind, have adverse impact on the flight path of the bullet. Bullet's trajectory is parabolic. When the air is denser, the resistance of air increases, the bullet travels less distance, and it drops faster as it is dragged downwards by gravity. With the wind in the same direction of the flight path of the bullet, the bullet will travel faster and longer distance, moreover at different ranges the drag downwards will be reduced. Hence air's density and movement have tremendous impact on the accuracy of snipping the target.

The longer the distance the further the bullet will stray with the wind. The ability to feel the speed and the direction of the wind is crucial in adjusting the scope to compensate for vertical and horizontal shift thereby increasing the accuracy of the shot. In the case of the Insecthunter, his greatest challenge is feeling for stagnation in all movements – the environment, the subject and the photographer. Everything moves in reality. Breeze however slight moves leaves or branches, changing the location of the arthropods even if it is stationary perching on the leaf, with magnification of life size as in 1:1 or greater, the subject can disappear from the view finder with only a slight movement. The arthropods move too like any animate animals. Their movement is a wonderful sight to watch and shoot. We learned to appreciate their locomotion and their habits. The signature habit of the house fly is 'washing the hands' action. In fact, the house fly washes their hind legs too! It also rotates its head slightly when cleaning its proboscis and face. We breath and heart beats, these actions created minute camera movement. In order to reduce these movements, we have breathing technique that requires us to stop breathing while shooting with two-thirds of the lung inflated. We compensate and wait between the heart beat to shoot in stillness. That's how far one can practice to shoot clear macro photographs. So too the snipper wait for the in between stillness. The stillness of the mind and the consciousness of this stillness is where practice and the power of concentration can bring about. Meditation is a good way to attain this state of consciousness. Achieve stillness and our insect hunting will improve.

Guilt and freedom

In the Microworld, the subject is always in constant motion, each expression is different, such as lifting the limbs, swinging the feelers, dropping poo, flapping the wings, stridulating the wings, moving the palps or fangs, twisting the head or celophathorax, lifting the abdomen and moving the genitalia. All these are wonderful and amazing expressions of the arthropods. They means something for the camera and the viewers, resembling and echoing some humanly behavior that we exhibit in public or in private solitude. There is no outrage of modesty in their nakedness and copulation, but for human, treading across this boundary requires societal acceptance, otherwise we will be sanctioned . There is absolute freedom to pursue our interest with the arthropods; their only defense is fleeing from our gazes. Killing them, terminating their life, because we have the power is the least thing we should do, unless our life is being threatened. As would with any human being, respect thy enemy and treat them with care, we would gain their respect and trust. Confucius once said that do to other as you would expect others to do unto you.

The guilt of killing a life, the feeling of seeing death, empathizing their sorrow and becoming the sorrow, hurts the shooter. He finds it increasingly difficult to cope with his action or inaction to save life. Self-introspection, self-accusation, shame, isolation and hopelessness, cause depression, and he may eventually take his own life. Kevin Carter, the Pulitzer Prize photographer, famed for his Vulture Stalking a Child, accused by some as a predator for a worthy shot was another vulture on the scene, as he was not helping but stalking the child and vulture for the infamous shot, unable to face multiple other difficult situations in life, he choke himself with carbon monoxide from his vehicle. He was a destitute, dejected, desperate, misunderstood, haunted, traumatized, a victim of a problematic world who eventually succumbed to Posttraumatic Stress Disorder, as would Daniel according to Penny Coleman. These are the haunting truth of photographers who seek truth in extreme human conditions, sick societies with human ills, which are too much to bear, as they continue to live the situation after making those photographs. They are sacrificial heroes. We salute them. We felt strongly such situation when the subjects are fellow human being, we relate better to their conditions on photographs without the trauma. For documenting the life of neglected critters, we were not able to feel such immense sorrow, interestingly, we felt their happiness or rather we associate nature with the magical power of love, power to cleanse and power to cure our psychological imbalances and imperfections. The minuscule amount of blood and inaudibility of the scream do not impressed on our senses to complete a sense surround experience, so much so that we do not feel their condition. We take pleasure in their sorrow; they do not complain aloud; they do not splatter huge amount of blood. Visual and auditory silence, silent our conscience, silence us, retain our peace of mind, blinding our emotion, we are calm. All grossly scene are masked out and muffled. There is no emotional trip to jolt our existence, waking us from numbness of this everyday life. Shooting the critters, is the making of a single frame movie, a shorthand of sort, a cliché, a fad, emotion is condensed and summarized in a single pictorial landscape that is presented for repetitive scrutiny. There are no suicidal urge but a wonderful feeling of life and glory. Such is the satisfaction, an immense love for life, including death. Great fulfillment is derived from appreciating and discovering the vast pictorial landscape of the Microworld.

Breathing and liberation

Everything is in motion and in a constant flux. When we sat there motionless meditating and sensing our body and rhythm, we will sense our breathing. As we breathe in, the air flows through the nostril, into the phalanx, down the wind pipe, fills up the lungs and expands into the diaphragm. We could hear our heart beating. However slight this constant movement is, it never stops as long as we are living. As our anxiety rises, the heart beats harder, the breath becomes shorter, and we may even vibrate involuntarily. All these bodily reaction will affect the accuracy of the shot when the sniper is zeroing in on his target before he decides to squeeze the trigger. This slight movement is magnified in the view finder, the image rise as we breathe in and lower when we breathe out. Stillness, calmness, and concentration reduce movement and increase accuracy. In fact, the bodily movement has to be taken into account; it has to become constant such that the movement is predicted and the shift is accounted. Skillful sniper is known to shoot in between heart beats. The way to be still and calm is an art which has to be perfected and its perfection enable one shot one kill. At that crucial moment, all consequences of past and future dematerialised; the concentration of now is the only existence. Here lies the essence of life, now. When we understood that this moment is, we live the fullness of time and space. All thoughts of past and future are wasted time, as our consciousness wonder astray and we are not living in the now which is real. Thoughts of the past and future are not real as they remain as thoughts in our consciousness, though they are so real in our mind. Most events do not unfold accurately as we have planned and imagined. They happen incidentally and accidentally. Loose those past emotions of hatred, anger, grief and uncertainty, be aware of the now, the present, feel every breath of this moment, concentrate on this life. That is the same instance when the camera and the Insecthunter becomes one, the sniper and his rifle become one, the sniper sees only his target, both depress the trigger to kill the moment and accomplish. They learn and realize that life is worthy only when this moment is lived in this moment. They felt every space of this moment. Time is non-existence. Eternity is made.

How does a sniper live with his guilt of being the executioner, of playing god, of killing for his country and money? He could hardly been able to reconcile, the confrontational image when his shot hit his target. He begs for reconciliation with his guilt in the silence of the night. Nightmare in his own lonely existence replays often in his sleep or for some drench drunkard in his intoxication. What is his salvation? Or is he doomed? They fight for the ideology of others and face the greasy guilt that is illusively haunting. The insecthunter, enjoys the thrill of shooting, but without the guilt, in fact, by bring the image to the world, he helps to raise our awareness of insects and spiders, and he promotes natural living and a sustainable environment. Most of all, he chose his believe and he is a free soul, owing nothing to anybody or the world, except he has to find a way of sustaining his livelihood. A good sniper is well decorated and his pension provides all those material he needs to sustain him. However, the hurt he carries with him requires cure that money cannot buy. A way of coming to terms with the necessary evil of this world will rid him of his guilt and he will then find peace within.

Though both kill, the difference between the photographer and the sniper is, one image is written eternally internally, the other is written eternally externally that could be shared and communicated with an audience. Both felt strongly the effect of their accomplishment. One is melancholy and pessimistic, the other naively celebrating life and wonder. Both are seeker; they seek a needle in a haystack, making that single shot count, regardless of the difficulties they would face, they could overcome them.

Seeking

The seeking is thrilling and a lonely affair. The path of tracing the subject, when described would seem like madness, a sniper crawling and inching towards his subjects for kilometers and days. Everyday's insignificant affairs such as eating, sweating and excreting, become enormous and arduous, unthinkable for us. The Insecthunter stalking the arthropods in the bushes, sometimes squatting, crouching, standing, bending over, or spreading out, making only slight movement of millimeters for hours, looking utterly insane to the uninitiated. That madness makes greatness. Both would be proud of relating the event leading to the accomplishment, one would abbreviate the imagery of the kill for the pain it contains; the other would expound the beauty in the final moment, the eternal image that iconized the subject. They are both a loner. They face fear alone. They overcome their fear and themselves alone. They are destined to loneliness as they have chosen their calling. God save them!

However tense is the final moment, their mental state would have to be still and calm. Sniper would have to face death calmly, either his own or that of his opponent or both. He respects his enemy as much as he respects his own fellow brother in arms. He kills to save lives. His own safety is the least of his concern. Stillness and momentary stasis is required at the brink of making the kill. The sense of making the final moment would usher a sense of relief, an end to this arduous journey and days of loneliness. However, pulling out and withdrawal may not be as easy as we would have envisage, but it is crucial, to live up to the art of the sniper, he who shoots and runs away, lives to shoot another day. Searching for that stillness is also crucial in insect hunting, Peering into the view finder, everything moves, even small minute movement would render the image blur or outside the framed view. Breeze however slight also affects the image. There are always breezes. We see them moving the environment, the leaves, flowers, branches and the flickering shadow. The triggering is made in the momentary stillness that lies between the breezes. It would have to coincide with the perfect being, dramatic lighting, and precise focusing. Sweat would stream down the face and part along the eyebrow ridges, increases the humidity in the still air and traps the breath between the camera back and the face, between the butt and the scope, rising to affect the vision and appearing as condensation on the view finder. Vision becomes blurry and the image distorted, fluctuating between sharpness and vagueness. Any triggering at this point, is a gamble, there is no way to guarantee the exactness of the shot under this condition. Everything has to be crystal clear, breath calm and mindful to nail dead the kill. The trick is to look away for awhile or close the eyes for a split second before taking aim again. See the target clearly, postulate and release the kill. Intense concentration may constrict the muscle of the body and holding still other functions generates a lot of body heat. There is always profuse sweating and strain on the muscle as they have to lay motionless. Blood may not flow in certain areas and prolong inactivity would induce numbness, pain and discomfort in those area. For the Insecthunter, focusing at close distance is not about twisting the focusing ring or using the autofocus dial. It is about setting to manual focus and moving the body forward and backward ever so slightly. The slightest movement is made by moving the body about the hip while the posture of holding the camera stilly has not changed. A light and small monopod, similar in function to the bipod, is an added advantage for increasing accuracy and stability. With more stability, image shot can be sharper at slower shutter speed, lengthening exposure time, and allowing movement to be written on the same photograph. Here we can see stillness and motion in the same image, capturing a living being within a dead space.

Simplicity – one camera, one lens and one shot

Simplicity is beauty. This is true with the use of camera. The equipment needed for the shooting is a simple set of camera with a single lens, a lens hood without the filter, as filters reduces light and affects optimum performance of the lens. There is no necessity to carry many lenses or camera bodies. Stooping in the bushes with a lot of equipment scares away the insects and spiders, slow down and impinge on movement and maneuverability. Usually for less than a day's travel, a litre of water and some chocolate snacks is enough to keep the hunter going. For a little more stability, a small and light monopod would suffice. Using existing light would further reduce the weight of the equipment. The use of ring flash, or dual flashes increase the overall size of the equipment and accessibility to the insects. They would be scared away as a huge bulk approaches them. One camera, one lens, one shot and one kill is the motto towards insect hunting.

Apricot

Where does the sniper take aim to lessen the suffering of the hunted, the point of instant death, the least he could be merciful for his deed, a consolation he gave himself as no one would be there to console his guilt or lessen his grief of terminating life, the wonderful gift of, nature, or for some, god. God gave life and the power of his creation to take what he had given, how strange of him or generous of him, that we have the power to do evil. The merciful sniper takes aim at the 'apricot' or the medulla oblongata, the part of the brain that control involuntary movement, which when shot at, delivers instant death, painless and preferred, or assume to take preference over a suffering death or painful death. This point of interest is always at the centre of the aiming scope for the sniper, but for the photographer, or the classically trained photographer, it is two third or one third to centre or the left or right of the hunted, a composition known as the rule of third. However, the camera makers still prefer to locate the focusing point right at the centre, demanding that the photographer take a two step approach to focusing and compositing, in the process, leaving a clue in the image to inform us of the expert from the casual. Only in very rare occasion a centralised composition would be deployed by the expert. In portraiture, as in the portraiture of the arthropods, the traditional point of focus is the eye. The eye is the window to the world of the individual, the sparkle exudes life, without which it indicates death, a reflected white spot in the black of the eye would be found in all portraits. Portrait painter would add white dot here to give it life. Focusing on the eye is also crucial when shooting for the portraits of the arthropods, unless it wasn't their portraits that one is after, again a two step approach, focusing and compositing.

The hunter and the hunted

Getting into position to have a clear view of the subject requires careful planning and selecting the vantage point where the target will be clearly seen and the view should be perfect for taking a clear shot. The sniper is always hiding. He does not give away his position, he deliberately conceals himself, covers his trace. The sniper can be hunted by another sniper. His is a life and death situation, as in all warfare it is an achievement to come back alive and be decorated. The Insecthunter has no way to conceal his presence from the tiny critters; he is too huge to be concealed. The critters constantly sense the movement of the environment, leaves, branches, wind and light variations. They are alerted by sudden changes and react to them readily. They will be oblivious of the Insecthunter if he moves like the environment, and becomes part of the environment. The lens, a giant obtrusive device, intrudes into their space, hovers over them, cranks and shoots them. The Insecthunter is at liberty to shoot from all angles, except his movement has to feel like part of the environment. Slight movement changes the angle and view point greatly. It is easier to make view point changes, but to change it slightly; it takes a lot more precision and effort to move so little.

Images shot with flash have a different feel and clarity. The image is harder, having a wider depth of field, sharper and crispier, but somehow lack naturalness. The color is richer and more saturated and have a certain punch to it. The form, texture and color of the arthropods are clearly shown, the details are intriguing and vivid which provide a good biological and anatomical study. Regardless of whether they are the grotesque or the beautiful they are given equal importance. Most often the flash has to be softened with paper, foam or plastic add-ons to reduce the glaring contrast and prevent wash out in high-light area. With the flash, aperture can stop down to f16 or f22, resulting in greater depth of field. As the flash has duration of less than a millisecond, it freezes and cast every moving being into stone. I prefer existing light, which looks more natural. However, the aperture will have to larger and strong sun lights becomes crucial.

Understanding the camera equipment.

Since young, I had a bacchante for using existing light to my advantage and have been adept at it. The discomfort with additional flash light, and preference for agility and maneuverability, made me commits to existing light macro photography. This has the added advantage of less investment in lighting equipment and accessories. It further reduces the amount of variations I have to grapple during shooting, allowing me more time and space to focus on the subjects. In the process, I develops a keen eye for seeing light and shadow, and positioning the camera to achieve better results.

It was said that a true photographer would always need to have his camera with him. That the precious moment would perhaps flee and gone when it was not recorded.

Seeing

Most often than not, you would have been told that some photographer sees the images in his mind and go on to create the great photographs he had envisioned. Yes, looking back, we all did have that mode of creation, for that image which we was extremely satisfied and we would tell ourselves, yes, we had finally been able to synchronized and made real from the mind into print, that we had arrived at precise creation at the moment when we depressed the shutter, we knew, we had that image eternalised as in our mind. We would poured in many hours of darkroom work, making development of negative and printing, a precise science. Only through understanding details and necessity of the detail processes that we finally arrive at certainty. This was only half of the equation to the image making, the other, was the mind's visualization, precisely what would be the same as that eventually made permanent on print. This would require many hours of practice and understanding. Photography would seem to us as the Art of Science, neither art nor science alone would suffice, only the gifted would have mastery of it. The photographer was mystified as having that extra power of visualization, almost godly that not all human beings could achieve.

However, with the introduction of the digital camera, the camera makers are in full force to destroy this myth that many great photographer held on dearly. Would digital camera and LCD screen help us see clearly and precisely the images we are about to create. It seems far from it. We seem to see something better, but there again the images on the LCD are also a reproduction, which when view on different displays or printed from different printers are not the same. The same precision, required of art and science, still eluded us, even more so with the digital equipment as there are so many ways to tune the same display. Every equipments has to be tuned or controlled, including the environment which we are viewing them, would render the images differently. Under different lighting condition, for example, under natural daylight or florescent lighting the same print appears differently. For those unacquainted eyes, they may not see the differences, the events or the subject matters on the print takes precedence.

Has the making of a good photographs becomes more difficult? Or even simpler? How can we measure the quality of greatness in a piece of art? Is it difficult? Any expression would just be a subjective endeavour and very difficult to quantify. It could just generate more urban myth that we do not need great photographer any more, everyone can be a greet photographer with a digital camera. Most often then not, this is not true. Importantly a good photograph is the reflection of the photographer's thought. He positioned the camera, arranged the lightings or select the lighting condition of his preference, framed the image, controlled the exposure and snapped at that particular moment, within that instant there are multiples variations. It would be quite impossible, with so many variables that two different individuals would create the same image at the same place or events. That is the charm of photography, the impossibilities of creating the same copy, even taken that all other variation could be duplicated, and no two cameras can occupy the same space. It is a truly one and only original possibility, none to others.

This is a copy of reality, the camera, like a cloning dcvicc, clones a piece of reality at that particular moment, make permanent as an authentic record of reality and the proof of occurrence.

The thrilled in the search for the insects and spiders is that, one does not know what could be found, the happenings are coincidence, like the chance encounter of the sewing machine and the umbrella, pure chance, without prejudice and one's preference. One do not need to stroll the street of Paris, gathering that chance encounter and creating that surrealistic prove, propagating Freudian and Bretonian thought, of the subconscious and autonomous nightmare, as the Dadist and the Surrealist had faithfully painted, giving rise eventually to the super-realist painting, intending to better detail reality than photography could do. Here, Parisian landscape for the alter-reality is in our back guard, falling within a small area of less than a food ball field, and if you like raise the limitation to a ten metre square, explore till death, as the ultra-modernist would do, the world of dramas conducted by the insects and spiders, and the possibilities and coincidences are beyond our imagination. It is life, changeable, malleable, accidental, murders, birth, growth, maturity, celebration, grief, exhilaration, beauty, ugly and more, endlessly duplicating with slight variation towards eternity. An unending story that can be recorded and duplicated, and yet they never cease to excite our emotion and fascination. If Matise is in the tropics, presumably the diversity of live would have a huge impact on his pictorial landscape.

Each image, brought with it the tradition of thoughts, past, present and future; it prejudices and liberates. We see and are blinded by their beauty.

5. History and potentiality

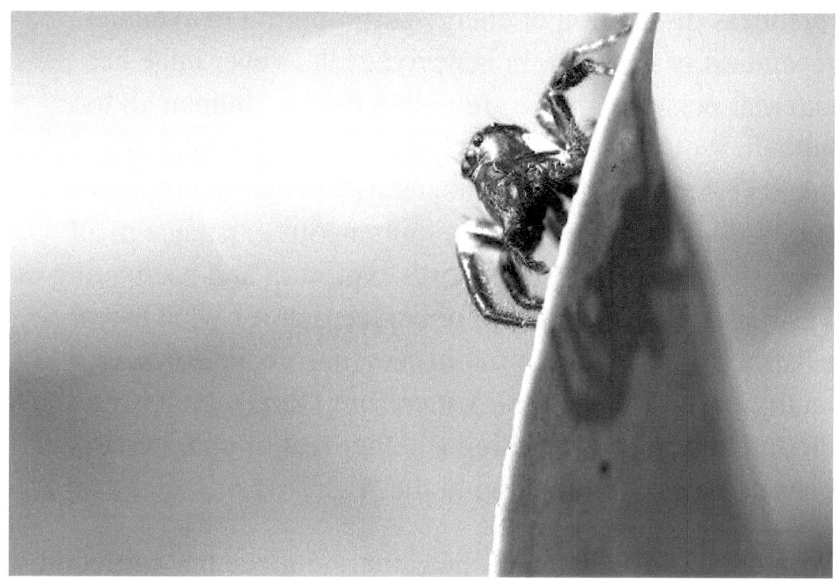

The portraitures made by Avedon of remarkable personalities, captured a certain epoch iconographed by his subjects' persona, and yet we see that split second of vulnerability, which Avedon, a hunter, armed with the ability to slice through that thin moment, laser sharp, made eternal that particularity of emotion, returning them to their humane existence, the susceptibility of fear, rejection, despair, and bewilderment, re-establishing their trivial existence commonly found in any humanly being. Avedon's Marilyn Monroe, the highly charged sex symbol, was caught in the glimpse of exhaustion, contrary to her famous cliché image of dancing with flaring white skirt, dynamic, youthful, energetic, immortalized by Matty Zimmerman. We, the mortal souls, have our moment, of a publicly upheld persona and a simpler definitive existence. This duality exists in everyone, you and I, however simpler our beings are. This duality, had a simultaneous existence in Avedon's Marilyn

Monroe, it is both historical and ahistorical; she marked the era of woman's emancipation, sexual liberty and her relentless dissipation of energy surmounting in eventual revelation of tiredness in her privacy, however huge her external persona, she is, after all, a human, human all too human. Would any arthropod in their being have that duality? Are they outside this nature? Is the rule of nature singularly pervasive, with a simultaneous existence in all beings? This is a question worth exploring and psotulating. Yes fantasizing, would you not agree that for what is real, exists a priori in our consciousness, before we perceive it in reality or our reality. I think therefore I am, such powerful dictum that trace everything whether real or conjured to our consciousness, terminating in the 'I'.

Would the introduction of the camera, induce the arthropod to perform, to straighten up and put on a perceivable 'I would like to be seen persona', as would most mortals? Is this occurrence pervasive in arthropods or particularly prominent in certain order of arthropods? Perceivably this trait would be more alarming in actors and actresses.

Jumping spiders, known as the family Salticidae, have huge frontal eyes attached to armor like heads that reminiscent German tank, sturdy and invisible. Each jumping spider, like most spiders, except some Spitting spiders have only three pairs, has four pairs of eyes. The other eyes by the sides and above the head are smaller. Jumping spiders are hunters that prowl the leaves and pounce on their preys; they are carnivorous. Of course, there are exceptions, like the iridescently coloured jumping spider, which I have noticed, feed on pollen or nectar. In fact I saw one scuffling with an ant for a white crystal and he was robbed of it, as that ant had stronger jaw and strength, I would assume. Jumping spiders are known to be friendly and inquisitive, especially the heavy jumper, a breed that has plenty of minuscule hairs. He was the first arthropod that impressed me and attracted me to spiders. I developed a liking for them and my familiarity with them grew fondly. They are like small little puppy. Whenever, I approached them, they would sense my presence and raised their head, turned and faced me squarely. Sometimes they would hop onto my camera or lens. I would then searched for them, blew lightly on them to reduce their activeness, as they would shrivel and withdraw their limbs, remained stationary for a slight moment, before leaping on their feet again. In that moment, my fingers and palm would be placed next to him and he would land on it. I would then transfer him back to the blade of leave where he had wondered off. I learned to handle Jumper when I was young, back then there was a craze for Fighting Spider. It was a favourite fun time and pass time to challenge and set up fights with Fighting Spiders among children and teenagers. We own our own fighters, had a strict diet for them and trained them to fight.

The prominent character trait of the fighting spider is that they love to fight. When two males meet each other, they would go into a trance like dance, made semi-circle around each other, sized each other up, charged at each other, and snapped both front legs in a frantic horizontal movement, sometime they fight till one died or one's limb was bitten off. The looser would run away and the other would give chase. We would declare triumphantly the winner. Is not fighting a savage trait that we all inherited when we were born, as a skill of survival, gaining the privilege to be here, in this being of presence? Through history, we could see that intelligence and art, is a form of decadence, savage and brutality is the skill needed in the preservation of the specie.

The Mongols and the Qing, ruled over the far superior civilisation of the Song and the Ming. Similarly the Fighting spider would have a better chance of survival compared to the less aggressive spiders; however some are supplemented with special arsenal, such as the Spitting spider, he spits out silk web coated with poison in split second, like a fisherman casting his net. Their inherited trait becomes our game and enters our collective memory, a personal history that would refresh our recollection of our experience as children re-establishing our previous existence.

Would we be able to record the history of the arthropods, an independent history or otherwise its history relative to our being? Have we ever seen a massive war conducted by one insect against another? Most of us would have. We could not understand the feud between them, but we could see one of these episodes play out in documentary; they recur.

Everyday there are so many births and deaths, as well as the continuum between them. Hardly any being, animate or inanimate could escape, the trinity: birth, being and death. Their histories are so insignificant to us, perhaps due to the lack of perceivable connection between ours and theirs, or perhaps their occurrence was predictably replayed with such certainty that we call them behaviour. History with certainty becomes a pattern, a definite thing, a triviality. Would each episode be exactly similar? Very Unlikely. However, at macro level, a blurring of the particularity recalls only the certainty of the event. Our inability to see them in detail, their minute nuances, nor even recognising their differences, nor identify this spider from that spider, we would not be able to postulate their history. They look predictably similar. Would this generality present itself when we zoom into them in the computer? It was unlikely that anyone could have acquired that sensibility to tell them apart by their faces even after repeated scrutiny. Would you be able to empathize the sorrow faced by the loosing spider, or the pride of the winner? As I recall, their identity could possibly be found in their movement, peculiar within each, slight variation in shape and colour, or their deformity, but seldom could we be dead sure of their identity.

Perhaps the history in fighting spider is derived from the history of human vanity, as most of us would be emotionally attached to their fighting spiders during younger days; this is enthrallingly worth conscious exploration. It had become the collective memory of the post Second World War generation, the baby boomers. Spider had become the preoccupation of school students after studies during the seventies. Fighting spiders had a huge following, they had a star status within captivity, we were their trainers and they are our pride. We felt like looser when they had lost the fight. However, not all are lost, we would devise ingenious methods to make them better fighter, change the training methods or their diet. All else fail, we would go into the bushes and try to capture another fighting spider, in the hope of discovering a brilliant fighting star.

We see the winner as the conqueror, worthy of care, good food and rigorous training. Feeding them red ant was a no-go, they would developed scratching action; they behaved more panicky, meek and less robust when meeting their opponent. A huge house fly would serve as a more potent meal. It energise and strengthen them. Training could be sparing with a lesser opponent.

Fighting was a male spider affair, we had hardly seen female fights, and they seem disinterested. The primordial instinct of gaining a wild increase in strength and fighting dexterity, was enticing the male with the female. It had an immediate impact on the psychology of the male spider, we had thought so. We learned how to 'fuck spider'. It sounds so obscene. If someone asked you to go fuck spider, he meant, buzz off, go entertain yourself with that meagre ritual – a derogatory terms. Yes, it was a ritual, albeit a sexual one, between a male and female spider. You may think that the person fucking the spiders, is both the audience of sort, a pimp with the desire to win, the match maker, a warp mental that peeps at sex show and the organizer of pornographic show. None of that went through our mind, we saw it as a way to win back the fight. Perhaps, today when a nerdy student saw it, it was science and he would be posting that eternal question and possibly turn it into a project, operating them with minuscule utensil, searching their dead body, imaging that flow of fluid from one area to another, postulating their reasons and affirming his thesis. However, this seems a lesser joys for those raw savage survivors, who held on to the spider trend, we preferred the enactment. In amazement, perhaps some kids would imagine the electrifying effect, that of between their father and mother, for the adventurous they might start wondering and enacting the same ritual upon their perceived lovers. Yes, they would affirm that they were electrically charged and vigorised, there was an invincible potency; they felt strong, and savage. Was it a myth? Later, we realised that though it invigorate, it tired you out, you need rest, only after rest, deep sleep, you would awake with renew confidence and positivism. Another, human legend, that we experience, and would not discount its impact, with male chauvinism, we would deny all science and affirm its impact, it is potent and we need them! Hurray to great sex!

When we first saw it, we were enthralled, questioning, interpreting and creatively verbalising the exactitude of the male being charged up by the female, as we could see the lifting forelimbs, bend in a 'C' shape, vibrating in ecstasy, as he touched the head of the female. Only the looser got to fuck, a concession, a sexual booster, to gain sexual prowess, turning them into that raw brutal energy needed in all fights. He went into a trance, vibrating, moved backward, then forward again, touching, vibrating, and the pimp would intercept his desire, and stopped short, disallowing the completion of the ritual. Now entered, the male opponent, it could be a rematch, which he had lost before, but with this prior sexual ritual, we saw renew vigour in his fight. We had seen a looser, became a winner, after the ritual, affirming this age old myth that sex instills instance power, nature is pervasive, we see similarity in human. For those that constantly win the fight, we would not allow them to mate; their youth and vigour would gain strength and last longer if they are célèbre. The Chinese did the same to rooster by removing the male reproductive organ, the rooster would grow bigger and the feathers are more colourful and vibrant. Onc wonder if someone invented a machine to sterilise the fighting spider, will anyone game enough to try the machine?

Here is an age old believe that spans a few thousand years of Chinese wisdom. Here is the modality of the spider's sexual ritual orchestrated by the human. After gazing at it and asking long enough, we found the answer. Where did the increase in strength come from? From his anger? Spider does get angry? Spider has emotion? So let's get him angry and may be he could fight better? So the denial of sexual completion got him angry? Let him be hungry and due to the lack of food, he could be more desperate and angry too, but then where would the strength come from if he had no food? Would he fight better, when food level is low? It had never been the method of choice compared to the sexual ritual. The male spider had multiple orgasms, Whenever his forelegs vibrated in the air, so we believe, and he believed too. However, he was prevented from ejaculating; the palps would be charged up, with immense 'oom'. The same energy was to be released in the fight. Here is where the similarity with the Taoist and Hindu sacred practise, that the sperms contain such immense energy and life force that it should not be released and be wasted during the human sexual engagement. They should be preserved, that is, ejaculation is bad. In fact, without ejaculation, the male can, through various means and practise, redirect the energy back into the body, re-assimilated, resulting in an increase in the health of the male, in the same process, he could have multiple orgasm, longer sexual engagement and it would be much more fulfilling for the female. Could the same potency happen, as could the spider? Would the image of the fighting spider, or any photograph for that matter could, with certainty, have that potency to continuously arouse emotion from its viewer? You would want to capture it, present it, and conserve it, create that potential in stasis.

The sexual ritual is history in the collective memory of that generation. If you asked someone, and they get elated about the fighting spider, you would know that they would be in their late 40s and 50s. Any Fighting spider photographed now, has the possibility to be anachronistic, in the sense that, they would recall the same history and memory of the past, regardless when they were shot, provided the background or context are not laden with the fragment of history, just an abstraction of green or brown. The image serves as a trigger, not a container of sign and meaning, as the memory resides in the viewers who had experience that era. Or perhaps this collective history could be deposited in books or oral history.

'The Injured King', is a tribune to the great spirit of the fighter. He stood high and mighty, without fear of certainty or the unknown, he faced up to challenges as they would come to him. A few blades of leave are adequate for him to call his own and provide him the food he required. He roamed and ruled over them. He fend off any invader even if he would loose his limbs, and he did, two limbs were gone, but his posture of raised head and cephalothorax, shown him to be triumphant and the denial of his handicap. He walked in great strike, exhibiting none of the sign of weakness. I had not known of his handicapped for many years, until I scrutinised these images of him, that I realised this significant. Would you rather be an injured King or a handicapped? Most of us always see our handicaps and forgot our greatness, attributing inability to them. Stand up, I would say, face the challenge with bravery and naivety, the same would be true for me and you. STAND UP!

6. Meaning and Context

Images of street scene, especially those that take a wider view to include people, street and architecture, they recorded and documented, in a broad stroke, the life, history and culture of the place. The image is laden with trace of temporality and spatiality. Through the people's apparels, fashion, facial expression, architecture, signs and symbols, we could gather meaning and deepen our understanding of the image. There are multiple pocket of spaces where the mind and eyes could move, pause, fill up, ponder, investigate, relate, and enjoy, its photographic landscape is complex and multi-layered. We could from portrait, see emotion and gain a sense of history of the subjects, the background would further provide and situate the circumstances and reinforce contextual meaning to the image supplemented by the viewer's knowledge, collective memory and individual experience.

The portraits of the arthropod, when compare to human portraits with a white background, single out the individual, wipe out the clue from context, would present less relational information and knowledge as the human's face would with his/her skin colour, telling eyes, bone structure, teeth if it is revealed and the peripherals he/she adorned. All these particularities are absent from the arthropods. However, I suspect detail descriptions and information can be garnered from entomological studies; it could be possible to derive a greater sensibility and appreciation of the arthropods, making reading of the portraits of arthropods much more enjoyable, challenging and meaningful. Most often, the Arthropod's portrait is situated in plain, uniform and homogenous background, which is usually soft and out of focus, or it is enlarged beyond their real size that it is unrecognizable, and force the attention onto the subject matter. The features on the portraits are bound for reading with the need for acquired learning and interpretations. It is a new frontier awaiting to be trace from entomological studies, bridging and revealing its presence in the Arthropod's portraits. However alien entomological studies may seem, buried in them, are centuries of obscured and privileged knowledge that require popularization and deprecation into profane language such that it can be easily consume, understood and ultimately assimilated by the secular mass population. Immense sharing could then be achieved and raise the understanding of Arthropod and make known their relevance to us and the universe. Herein lies another alternative pass time and hobby for the young and the old; an healthy one.

Nature is our teachers. Learn from them.

7. After photographing

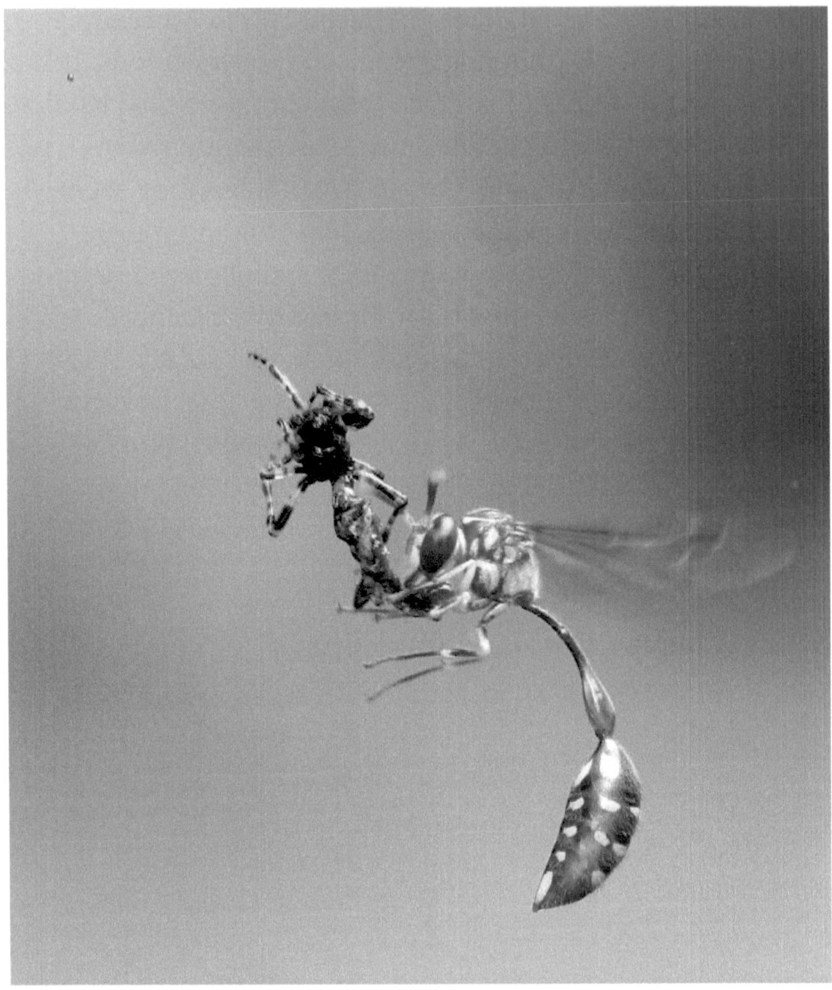

We tend to see more of an image, not in the instance we depressed that shutter, but persistently meditating on the meaning of life, of existence and being. Inherent in this image (The wasp is nibbling the Cyclosa) is the message of birth, being and death. When meditating on the image, the meaning unravels itself, in slow certainty, not in a flash, but a leap from normalcy, across the gap of invisible terrain.

Nights are always quiet, silence; days are a whole loaf of materialistic demands and bodily desires, that is the lure of the urban live. The night clears away those disturbances; we gain focus when darkness obliterated sight, reducing all existence to its essential. Only commanding a calm sense of ignorance, through sheer responsibility to the quest, silence could be found in daylight, with selfishness and irresponsibility required to overcome that momentous monster, social culture, a 'they' invisibly cajoling conformity, a slew of slogans of accepted goodness. Morality is borne from them, a form of coercion, to conform, to become, for the good of predictability and governance. Would we need morality when living in solitude and remoteness? Do we need morality when you are you. Or I am me. Would you think there is a need for morality in the social being of the ants and bees? Would you think that morality exists, or it is a mortal invention? And why all mortals think there is one, morality, and is it truth? What is creativity? Create, implies, new, leaping from the here and now to another landscape, non-conforming, difference, other than. And when creativity and morality collided, an immense nebular came into being, and when the nebular subsided, you rejoiced, like the nebular it too would subside.

With such monstrosity, with colorized lenses we could derive meaning and insight from behind each image we had taken. Exert values such as 'to kill is to sin' and we well up emotion of pity and a sense of injustice, from our righteous souls. 'Wasp nibbling in mid-flight' stirs the ocean of morality, jolts you. Imagine, you are the spider. In that silence, death grips you, you are as helpless as the spider, when face with the superior wasp, face with nature, face with fate, torned and tattered to the core, utterly helpless. If you are as omnipotent as god, you could right the wrong, but you, human – powerless, painful, and trapped. Trapped within a body and an illusive heart. You need liberation. You need a way out of this unfairness. Why? Why some are borne to die a tragic death? All are borne to die. Why the privilege of one over the other? You see the pain and the painless. What if your death gives life and meaning to other souls? Indeed, a good deed in death, over a painless unworthy death, is preferred. Yet, it is still death. Death has to be worthy! You scream in silence. You repeat. Death has to be worthy. Death has to be worthy. You scream in silence and determination. Death has to be worthy; life has to be worth living too. We latched on to its last defense, some are willing to die a worthy death, unwilling to believe otherwise, some see the futility of life, others see the futility of death, facing it squarely believing that it is the moment of returning to the source. All those thoughts are indeed a form of burden, death cannot be proven of its worthiness, all livings however they think and thought have to cease living at one moment or another when it come. Yes, nature's fairness, the being of beings.

Calm down, take deep breath, long and slow.

Remove the veil of morality, remove questions, and return to the surface of the image. Draw towards the wasp, trace the wasp, from the eyes, amazing red, glittering, energy, radiant, vitality, the mouth, the thorax, the flapping wings, in unison, the legs, the constricted waist, the abdomen, the curve, the pointedness, the texture, the pattern, colour, the minuscule hairs. Complete beauty!!! Such wondrous miniature contains life, being and death. It is so small and yet so complete. Complete! Life in this being, is.

The flapping of the wings in unison with the pull of the beaks, tearing the Cyclosa's remaining cephalothorax away from its head, the Cyclosa in its death had offered itself up as nutrients to the wasp and its offspring. The Cyclosa becomes the giver of live and sustenance so that the wasp could live.

Facing death, a mangled piece, a head, an eye pops, the placid legs, red, torn, see it, go through every nuance of it. Fear and the urge to escape gripped us. Fix on it and see it as you would see the beauty of the wasp. In death we find liberation. Unite both within a single instance. Life, being and death. The being of the wasp is to feast on the spider. A completion, closure, calm and peaceful. Nature is. Is wonderful. Here we see a completion of nature's work, again, in repetition - birth, being and death.

Why is death liberating? Imagine you are the spider. Imagine that dying moment, as death grips you, it erases all that you had done, it erases your worthiness, it erases you. Fear, extreme fear, penetrates you deep, deep into your soul, and erases your soul, erases your being, to the point of total erasure. You scream. Scream out your soul. See it vanished. Your denial is futile. You feel that cold sweat and coldness shrivel up the spine. All fears liberate when you die.

In death, nothing else matter, desires, debt, hatred, anger, anxiety, joy, love and all emotions; all vanished. One is forgiven and one forgives. So imagine you are the spider, in that instance, liberated, one gave its life to another being, there is no foe, enemy, nor love, just pure being, freeze in that moment, a singular moment. All is a pristine whiteness. Lost grips you, shaken, and arrive at a sense of immense liberation.

From that barren whiteness, a wasteland, life start a new, death nourishes beings and gives birth to another, more lives flourish, another time, another day, another month, another year, in recurrence, towards eternity. One sees its persistence and our futility of denial. It is an impossibility to phantom death, but we could phantom that death liberates. Life is a form of energy, transforming from one form into another.

The Cyclosa's death, had also liberated those that could had been captured by the web that was spun by the Cyclosa. Now those smaller animals were given a chance to survive and mature; they have the wasp to thank. As one lays down their power, whether destructive or creative, it allows others to flourish and mature. Those that had risen would have to fall some days, the sage cautions, in high places, serve with humility and in low places, serve with pride.

An image becomes more wonderful, when it was look at, searched and clarified.

Image has the power to clarify us, if only we seek them.

8. Framing

The camera, always frames the picture. We too always frame, focus on what we want to see, although we have a wider visual field, we constraint and concentrate our curiosity on a very small area of the visual field, sometimes zooming into one hundredth of the actual visual field. By this framing, we obliterate others. We obliterate other possibilities. It is a conscious act of framing, but what is that, that arouse our curiosity? How did that particularity caught us, capture us, and demanded our attention? Sometimes we are trapped by them, and to free ourselves, is to let it go. The visual field always consist of many disparate entities. Movement, always without fail, is the first that caught our attention. Movement is relative. Only when we are still we can see that others had moved, if one is always moving, he is unable to see movement if others are moving at the same speed. They look stationary.

To locate, to see, to feel, to hear, to smell, and to sense, is to keep still. It is in this stillness that present clarity. To appreciate, close your eyes, relax the muscle, feel the strain releasing from the skull, the eyes, the ears, the nose, the jaws, the shoulder, the arm, the hands, the fingers, the chest, the lungs, the stomach, the groin, the thigh, the culf, the feet, the toes, be a stone. Bring attention from the inside to outside, reach out, locate the sound, hear them, search the next, or stay, search behind, search the left and right, see with the eyes close, feel their vibrations, feel their stillness. Open the eyes slowly, see where your heart brings you. Look inward, see that you were obliterating other sounds when you were concentrating on one. Focus and concentration blinds and illuminate.

When you have stillness, you would see, things passing, things' presence. This is the best way to locate the insects and spiders. When you had not found that something, stop, pause, keep still, search inside and outside. Or if you just want to wonder, take an adventurous trip, find a spot and keep still, experience them as they appear. Contain in each of them is that same message of life. If you like, now lift your camera and make that image. Otherwise, you too had already made an image. These images can be shared in many ways and forms.

We are always framed by our height. It is natural for us to see around our natural eye level as we scout for the subject. Look up. Look down. Keep seeking and you will find something.

9. Observing

Shooting alone would not improve the image, non-shooting, meditating on the shot image, unravelling the hidden qualities, or unraveling our mind, installing thoughts in our unconscious mind, would sharpen our selection and framing of the scene when we shoot. Having meaningful images is not only about technically, but it is about how we see life and narrate it in our photographs.

Post processing, educating ourselves, imbuing thought into the image, educating others about our thoughts, our biases and privileges are the making of the image. Depressing the shutter, is only the beginning. We have to imbue life into the image and let the image take on a life of its own. Every photo has its own existential meaning and value.

Surrealism. arthropods are surreal, as we do not see them many times larger then their actual size. Some images of 1mm were even enlarged to 100 times so that we can begin to see them clearly, make some sense, relate to them and connect with them.

Images

Cicada

It was all rain for the last few days. I had been holding back from shooting. Trying very hard to finish up my writing for the book I had been preparing for a long time. Days were spent cycling in the morning to get the body ready, a routine, a ritual before, I sit down at the cafe for my cappuccino and a hamburger, then the brain start rolling, startup the eeePC and type.

The rain always bring surprises. It clears the air, laden sparkling diamonds on leaves, barks, wings of insects and the webs of the spiders. It is a spectacle. It brings life, clears and refreshes, without a doubt or grief.

I passed the park. The songs of the Cicada, stoled my attention, seduced me. Without hesitation, I dismounted, surveyed the trees. I found their molt. Imagine their mass migration from the wooded floor up the tree barks. Traced their songs and found many of them on the tree barks.

Cicada strangely love odd numbers. Their life cycles are marked in odd numbers. They vary from a few years to as much as 17 years. Those that sing are the male Cicada, the female are known to be quiet. Most of their years were spend underground, about a feet to three feet below ground, when they see daylight, their death are approaching. It is also their courting and mating period and it only last about a month. During which the eggs are laid and the parents both perished in death. It seems ironical. Love and death within such a short period as compared to their life span and their growth from egg to adulthood. I suspect there are more male Cicada then female Cicada, because whenerver I saw the Cicada, it sang.

Days gone by, without shooting, every often I passed them, I trespassed them, watched them and shared their joy.

This one day, I saw his sacrifice. I cycled home, grabbed my camera and returned to document this ritual, but it was too late, they were gone. His dead body could had been clean up by the weaver ants, and she had to find a place to lay her eggs. Natures' song of death and birth, alternating instantly from one to another. Their children will never get to see their parents. For human, we would never forgive our parents and regret if our parents are not there for us.

10. The Ant Death

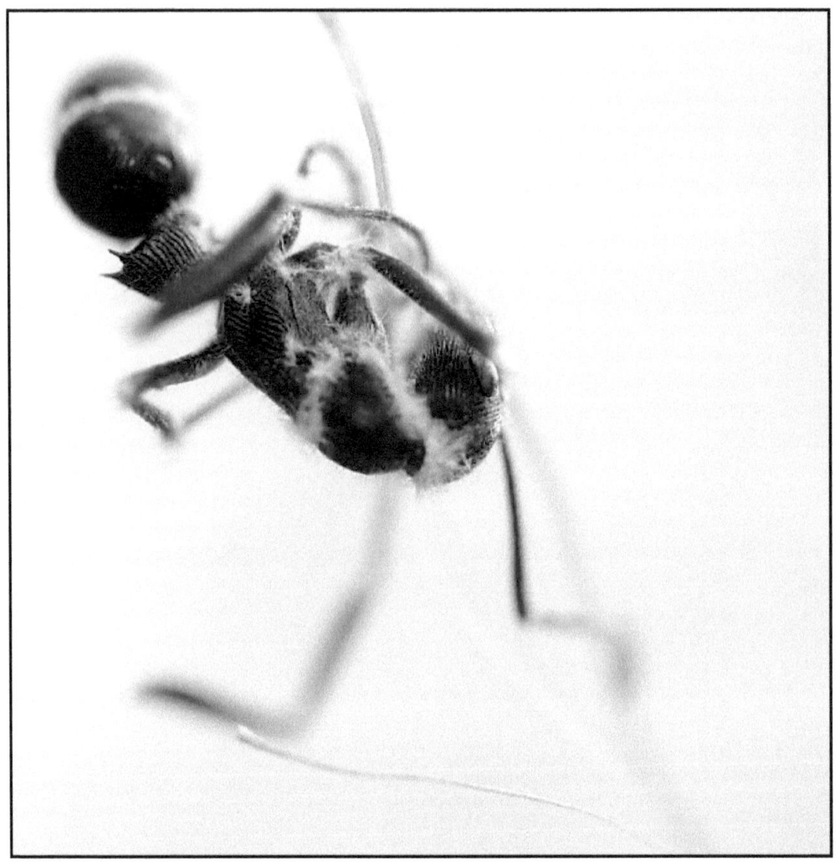

Death had been a subject which we explored frequently in our daily live, most of us would not like to come face to face with it, however through our journey on earth, inevitably we have to deal with it when it occur to our close ones, and eventually we have to face death ourselves. Death is the inevitability after birth.

Every living thing has to face death. He faced a slow death. Little by little the fungus germinated and fed on him. He had no doctor. No one who was able to provide medication or surgery to remove the invading parasite. Did he feel despair?

May be. Death would have taken over him when the fungus had engulfed his whole body. His only recourse was to climbed to the top of the plant, bit hard on the stem and waited for his life to be terminated. This is Nature. No right or wrong, no cruelty or sympathy, just being.

Death paints the triviality and fragility of every living being. Every sadness will come to pass if you see the nature in every things.

The ant prepared for his death. We are always aware of the peril and agony of disease caused by malignant virus and bacteria in human. Some times we forgot that all living things faced the same danger. Here is an ant engulfed by fungus resulting in his death. He too want to have a good death, to rise to highest tip of the stalk, bit hard and tight, remains in a stasis illustrating his unwillingness to succumb. Perhaps I read to much into his action, but why not, this image would resurrect the spirit of life and all living things, an eternal struggle against death and even face with its inevitability, we show our resolute.

My dad passed away many years ago had prostate cancer and he was in his last stage of a full blow symptom. He bloated because of the body's inability to get rid of water from his system. The hand ballooned. We knew that his end was coming. He hailed from a traditional family, he believed that a good death should be one at home surrounded by family members. So it was his wish to return home. Together with my youngest brother we arranged for an ambulance with life supporting oxygen tank and brought him home. He died upon entering the door to our home. He was surrounded by my mother and siblings. His wish was realized. We were so busy arranging for his death certification, embalmment, and death ritual. Only after a week, in the quiet night, relaxing on the sofa, I felt a sudden surge of sadness over his death. He was a great father who taught me about life and care a lot about me. His greatest was his ability to face difficulty in life with calmness, resolute and a sense of 'all is well'. We all know we need to face death. We need to die with dignity and we want a good death.

11. Another Ant Death

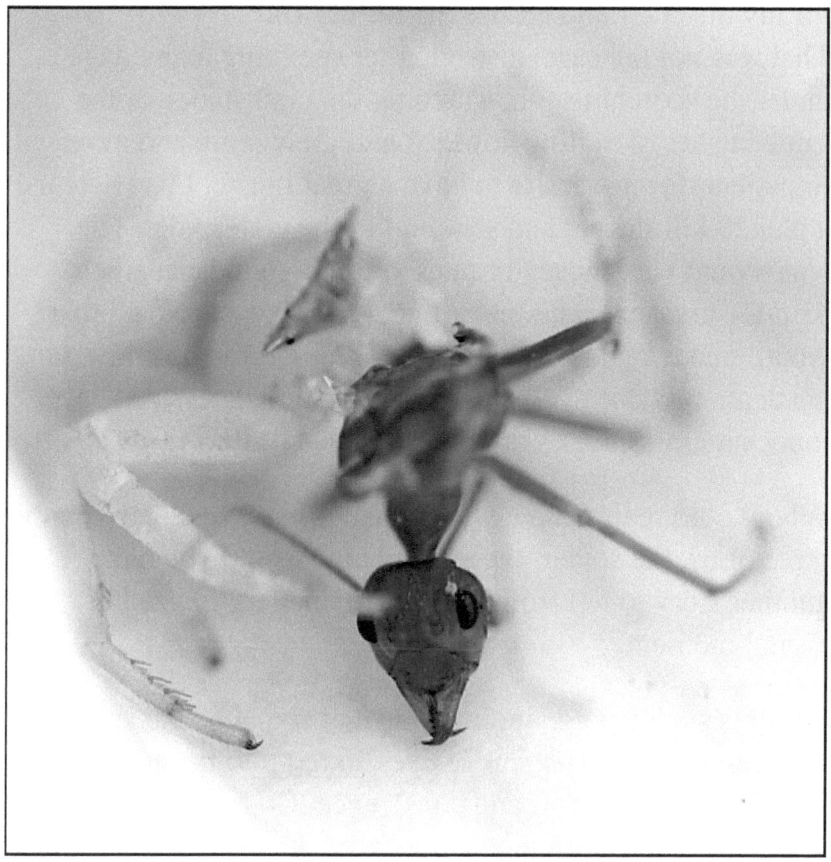

Here is a crab spider that is feasting on the red ant. I would have you believe that I stumble upon this occasion by chance and real hard work, scouting from flowers to flowers, my persistence was rewarded with this find. Death emancipating from the starring pairs of eyes, reminds you, makes you feel sorry for his death. There again, you felt helpless as this is part of nature.

But what if, I tell you that the ant was caught, injured and fed to the crab spider so that he can have a good feast. This was done in the moment when I was overwhelmed by the

long wait, together with the crab spider, that I took pity on her and started to give her some helps. Would you blame me for my mischief and accuse me for my sin?
That was not the case, instead, after spending many days under the scorching sun, watching the crab spider, at the same bushes of yellow flower, I had grew more and more impatient, for my desire to have a great image, I had hatched a plan to kill the ant and sent him to the crab spider. The weaver ant was chosen because of their abundance, their irritable nuisance, and their almost translucent red, all that would make a good compliment to the saturated yellow. On his death bed, his eyes starred into me and detested. The innocent crab spider was framed for his death.

Who would really know what actually happened between the three of us, the spider, the ant and me. Would you have another story to tell from this single imagery freezed in digital moment?

Death is such a poignant imagery that someone has to be held responsible. The pair of eyes stared into me and you, piercing into our heart and conscience. Conscience is one huge human creation that had its seed when we were young. Does nature has conscience?

12. More Ant Death

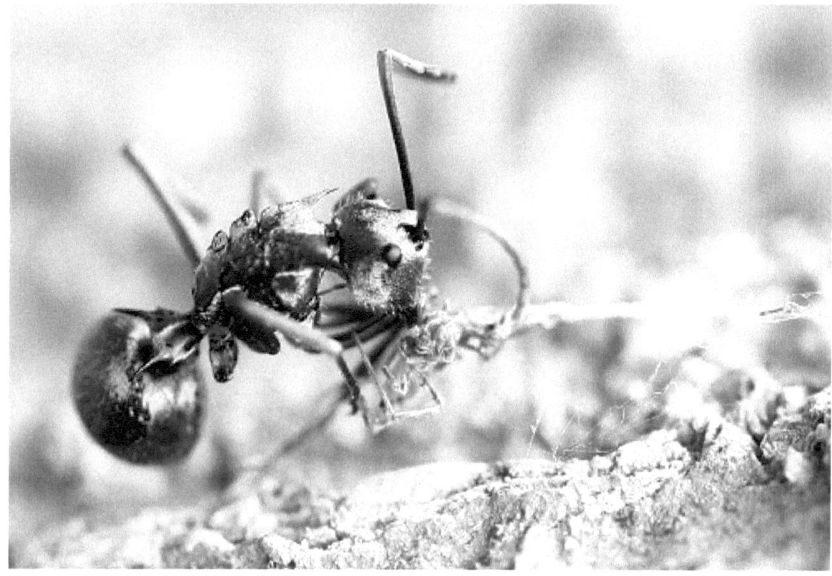

After reading Paul Arden's 'Whatever You Think, Think the Opposite', I was inspired to take some dead Insects instead of those alive and kicking. 'Photograph dead roses instead of the live roses which thousand of photographers had been photographing' kept ringing in my ears. So I spotted the most common of all dead insect – a dead ant hanging by a silk thread swinging in the breeze.

While I was photographing, I was constantly puzzling how did he died? Am I able to investigate the death of an ant? Interesting. It could make a good detective novel, unravelling the live of the micro-world. Am I autistic, like Mark Haddon had written? Who cares! I just want to be a kid again, pursuing the trivial.

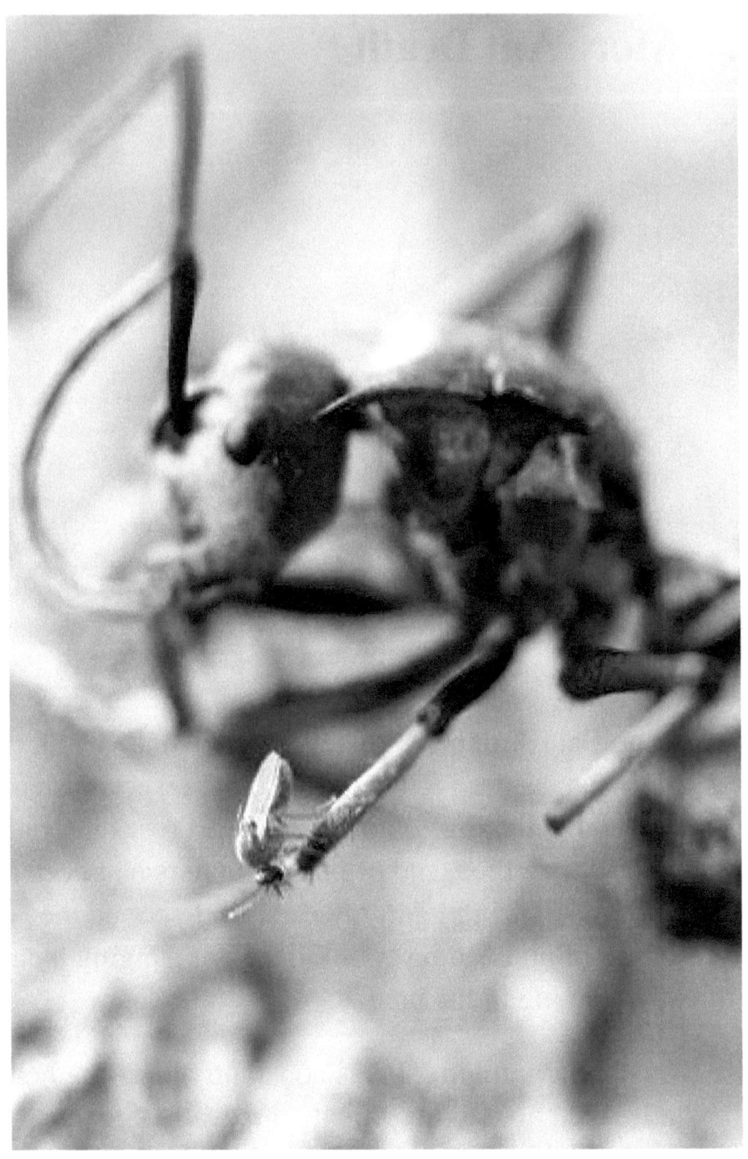

13. The beetle

Some how death had besiege this blue beetle, the fungus, or some kind of immobile living thing got over the mobile living thing. It sieged the beetle and locked him in this permanence. He left a stubborn blue shine as his illustrious venture. All things come and go others were made shorter by another.

Death trivialize every being.

14. Season

Every ten year or so, it seems, we will experience an economic down turn, we had the Asian Economic Crisis and the American Banking Crisis. They caused stirs in global economies. Cycles, Bell Curves and Maslow law are ever so applicable and useful to explain these phenomena. Human live an average of seventy plus years, in those years, many animals would had completed their cycles, we live to see their start to end, we knew their recurrence. The mosquitoes that were born in summer would not know winter; they died before its arrival. Seasons would have wiped out all those without ability to survive through winter; we call it natural selection.

However much we know about these cycles, many of us are not well prepared mentally and physically for their arrival, their creative forces and the flourishing opportunities they provide and the changes to be made. In one stroke, we see established and gigantic financial institutions collapse, schemers exposed, inequalities surface, restructuring of the banking systems, corporate death, scavengers benefited, voracious voices of protest, upheaval, political changes, administrative changes, then when all had subsided, the players and actors had changed, but the underlying power structure had not vary, society requires control and order. Seeing beyond the superficial fluctuation, we would find absolutism, the transient is relative and dynamic; this cosmological construct is the co-existence of duality. These artificial urban calamity, has its mirror, in the cycles of the vast tropical forest, every plants vied for the sun, the tallest tree perched high up serves the danger of being struck by lightning, when struck, it would fall, rot and provide nutrients to many smaller animals, such as termites, beetles and hoppers. The clearing created by the fall, provided sunlight for other living organism, kill others too, which are photo-phobic. There is a constant death and renewal. Cycles are eternal, as we would experience it within our cyclical limits. We could not live to see beyond the cycle, but we could phantom and alternate between linearity and its recurrence.

Within this recurrence, we worship and celebrate procreation, we are awed struck by that magical moment, when the female and male unite, a new life come into being, magical. Every living being are given that magical power, the power to create, regardless of richness or intelligence. On the forest floor, within a square inch, we could see life, the singular creative force is omnipresence.

Daily rhythm, seasonal rhythm, celestial rhythm,

15. Portraits of Arthropod

The 'Portraits of Arthropod' is a life long project that I had set up to pursue after I was awed by their myriad unseen world. They are mesmerizing and beyond what I had seen for 46 years. They were the least explored when compared to the world of the four-legged animals and the aquatic animals, primarily because they are tiny and we are not able to see them in detail unless we magnified them. Blow them up many times their sizes and we will realize they are as intriguing as the Dinosaur and as mystical as the phoenix we had never seen.

The project intends to observe and present their natural world, and with the belief that all living things are members of this home we call 'earth', the arthropods are treated as subjects with respect, care and understanding.

They are treated as another fellow human being, rendered in their, sometimes colourful, at times monotonous and excruciatingly cruel, natural environment.

Being true to the spirit of being natural, the photographing process did not employ artificial lighting, as in fill-in flash, setting up of their habitat nor putting them in captivity. The photographing process tends to be less intrusive, but observatory. Moreover they are neither treated as specimens nor photographed in great depth of field, but they are treated as a live model, explored in different angles, given focus on selected areas of their beauty. By diminishing the photographer's presence, all attentions are centred at making the minute large, in so doing, perhaps wish that the audience could gain interest and better appreciation of their world.

Documenting them in their moment is the greatest aspiration of the project.

I have to keep myself light and agile in order to track down the Arthropod and lessen the body load I carry. It allows me to concentrate on the subjects better carrying simple and little equipment. Tracking in the nature reserve or the garden, I always bring along my water bottle, which keeps me hydrated. Most of the photographs are shot in Singapore and a few in Malaysia. Dragonfly

I learned the behaviour of the Libellulidae by observing them. I realized that if I stay stationary when it leaves its favourite spot, it will return to the same spot and I can than inch slowly nearer it while holding my breath or breathing slowly without making too much air movement, continue to fire my shutter. Libellulidae, like most insects, is not alarmed by the clicking of the shutter, but by sudden movement. I was glad to have been able to get so close to it.

How could I capture that beauty of a fluttering dragonfly? I always asked myself. It was not until I saw them against the setting sun that I finally found that angel-likc wings flipping in the dazzles of flashing light. Yes, this made a perfect shot of that free-spirited beauty in Dragonfly. They flew against the softly blowing wind and in a seemingly happy movement, rising and descending a little, maintaining their position in the air.

In a sudden jerk it dived and clung onto the flower of the Heliconia. This is a perfect moment for me to capture it in its tussle against the gentle wind. I tried different shutter speeds and exposures, in order to achieve this image with the wings slightly blur in dashes of white; head and thorax in sharp focus emphasizing its determination and clarity of action.

Somehow, it was not easy to see their struggle against the gentle wind, but we saw the beauty in the struggle.

What would life be without that little bit of struggle? What would achievement be without immense struggle? Nature is a constant struggle. In that gentle wind, the dragonfly has to flutter its wings to keep its position, otherwise it may be blown away and landed on the wrong places. I once saw an unlucky dragonfly fell into the pond, struggled and attracted the fishes. In one huge gulped the fish ate the dragonfly. A slight slack can result in its sudden death.

Dragonflies are known to be friendly towards human; they are predators that relentlessly consume flies, gnats, bees, butterflies and mosquitoes. These "Mosquito Hawk" are known to be the greatest enemies of mosquitoes. At young age, as nymphs living in the pond, they already started to feed on mosquitoes' larva. They are fierce hunters in the air and can out maneuver their preys easily traveling between 30km/h and 60km/h, their flight are swift and more agile than those of any known birds. Their wings in its delicate structure works wonderfully in tensile stress, lifting the head, thorax and abdomen easily in split second. Dragonfly abilities to maintain flight in mid air and swoop down at its prey provided much inspiration for the helicopter invention. Igor Sikorsky, the father of helicopter, watched and drew inspiration from the Dragonfly.

We can learn from Dragonfly too, not just from its aerodynamic form but also from its strength in overcoming its weaknesses. In the tropics, the high temperature prevents the dragonfly to have long flight; flying heat up its body. Heat needs to be dissipated from underneath its wing, that explains why we see Dragonfly basking in the shade during a hot day or prolong flight, a process known as thermoregulation. This helps to reduce its temperature and balance it with the ambience temperature.

I watched this tired and 'hot' Dragonfly clung tightly onto the flower of the Heliconia. It had been flying for some time before taking that rest before me, however, the wind had become stronger and it had to constantly balance against the wind. Survival needs more than agility and skill; it needs determination. Its determination was commendable. It had to continuously change posture according to the wimp of the wind direction; angled its wings and tightening the claws helped to provide additional stability.

In this persistent struggle, it had to face another enemy, which had been silently nibbling on the wings of this Dragonfly and it had no ways to remove it. It may die in the hand of this parasite. We could see a small insect on the left wing of this Dragonfly just next to the thorax. It was probably less than 1mm in size; it could be a minute wasp or flea. I scrutinized all the photographs I had taken and found this particular one showing it clearly. The Dragonfly needs the wings to function excellently for it to catch its prey, without it, it may just starve to death. This is Nature, many were born and many will face death.

Holding a camera

16. One of the Primitive Residents at the Singapore Botanic Garden, the Mycetophilidae?

We spotted this insect hanging on a thread from a palm leaf at the Symphony Garden, (located in the Singapore Botanic Gardens). There were some transparent eggs above it. Its abdomen resembled that of a damselfly but it had a long proboscis and the eyes of a fly or wasp. The hind legs were long and gracious with spurs at the joints, the *Mycetophilidae*. I was shooting against the sunlight and made over exposure by 2EV to render the subject more visible bringing out the details. In the end, I got this image. It looked very much like a watercolor painting.

FAITH IS NEEDED

Locating an insect is about perseverance. After exhausting a particular locality, residence; visiting another, we will encounter alienation and unfamiliar landscape. A long search would ensue. Faith is the encouragement. The intense sunlight, which is needed for a satisfactory photograph causes immense discomfort, though we are grateful for its presence,. Sweat is profuse. A white cotton T-shirt can help to soak up the sweat. The sleeves are good to wipe off sweat from the face. We understand the greatness of light- weight equipment and our fully filled water bottle.

PERSEVERANCE WILL PAID OFF

Moving away from my favourite Tropical Rain Forest. I was determined to find new “models” among the palms at the Symphony Garden one morning in the year 2006. Anxiousness and optimism put me to a good start.

Eventually it was faith that kept me going. Among the palms we found a small insect that piled rubbish on itself. It was an extremely difficult subject. There were also spiders which were about 1-2 mm in size, minute, another difficult subject.

I changed tact, instead of scanning at eye-level, I started looking up and found something hanging. The subject, about 1.2 centimeter long and hung precariously on the thread from the palm leave. It carried some translucent eggs above it. I thought it was a wasp. I love its structure - curvy, aerodynamic, firm and austere. I was breathless. Extended my monopod to the fullness and tiptoed to gain extra height. A slight breeze made it sway. I had to refocus constantly. The lens was set to manual focusing. Focusing was in the form of minute movement of the body forward or backward.

All this while I moved cautiously, inching towards the subject. I started to perspire, intense concentration, regulated breathing and non-breathing as I triggered the shuttle. I realized through the length of the breeze, if one waits long enough, there is an intermittent stillness. I could almost hear the thumping of my heart. There is always this stillness among the ruffle. This was the chance to create that single frame of stillness and that stillness had to be in focus. The moment was so critical that I always wonder, was I always ready or was I plain lucky each time, or was it that I trigger by mere estimation, feeling or intuition? At the age of 44, I had shortsightedness and farsightedness. An handicap most will come to term with. Human faculties when acting in unison can over come personal shortcomings - synergy, Bucky (Buckminster Fuller) would have you believe that the end is greater than its sum. That was how he conceived the geodesic dome.

Anxiety ran high. Very Excited. Thrilled. I was shooting against the sunlight; I over-exposed to bring out the shadow details. I was so satisfied and repeatedly viewed through the selection, searching, discovering and perfecting the shots. I shot for almost an hour. All this while I had not seen it move. It was in deep concentration. Through the lens, I saw a gracious lady with a single arm, elegantly wrapped and clung effortlessly onto a thread, oblivious to the surrounding or danger. Its proportion was so heavenly. The long beak was unique. The colour was cool pastel. I sincerely and superstitiously believed that it was a vegetarian; most blood sucking insects are not colourful as they fed on processed food. Did we ever see a colorful mosquitoe that suck human blood? It was, therefore not a mosquito.

THE IDENTIFICATION, THE SEARCH.

It had to be a wasp. I searched the internet for similar insect. I found that a certain species, the *Bombyliidae*, spotted almost similar features. An insect that sucks nectar to survive. However, Urtica thought it was a Crane fly, *Tipulidae*. I compared the images of both and noted that there were differences in the beaks and the abdomens.

Omeuceu, quite an expert in identifying insects, had this to say, "I am pretty sure that this is not *Tipulidae* fly. *Tipulidae* flies have no spurs and the head configuration is very different. Order Diptera. This is not a damselfly, neither is it a wasp. It is clearly a *Dipter*" Omeuceu said that this is neither a *Bombyliidae* , "I am pretty sure that your fly is NOT *Bombyliidae*. The proboscis is very different comparing with Xespok's photo. It points downward in your photo, and it is much more longer than the other proboscis. It has spurs in your photo. *Bombyliidae* in the other photo hasn't."

The fly belongs to the order of *Diptera*. Since I started to photographs arthropods, I had refused to photograph flies though their huge red eyes are captivating. This prejudice was associated with a tropical disease that was transmitted by houseflies. Their hairy legs and their constantly washing their forelegs imprinted a nauseating disgust in me. This fly changed my narrow perspection of the Order *Diptera*. Wow, they can be so elegant and they could be herbivorous!

Another expert, Longristra said, "Due to the wing shape, antennae, eye structure, legs and abdomen, I would say this is part of the family *culicidae*, mosquitoes. Definitely not a mayfly. Mayflies hold their wings in a different position, have shorter legs, longer segmented antennae and most importantly, no feeding apparatus." Could it really be a mosquito, yet another disgusting insect. How beauty could be bestowed on such ugliness. Mosquito causes Dengue Fever in the Tropics, some people died from it. I did land in the hospital for a week due to constant high fever. It was believed to be Dengue Fever.

I sent emails to experts whom I found on the web. I had some astonishing replies. Matt Bertone of North Carolina State University said,, "I just saw that this is not from the Nearctic so it could not be *Lygistorrhina*. However, it is definitely accurate to say it is a member of the *Mycetophilidae*. Great Picture!" Wow! So what exactly is a *Mycetophilidae*. The name sound nicer now. I was more satisfied with this identification.

According to Wikipedia, *Mycetophilidae* is a family of very small flies, the bulk of which are commonly known as fungus gnats, as they feed on fungi. There are 3000 described species in 150 genera. They can be predators too. The only strange difference is the beak. I noticed that the fungus gnat has a shorter beaks. The end of the beak turns downwards slightly to make a small hook. It defers from the subject I had photographed. Its beak is slender and long, I thought it couldn't scrape fungi and feed on them. The beak looks like a sucking apparatus, I could imagine it sucking nectar.

Then I got a reply from Thaptor suggesting that it is not a fly in the zoological sense (Order Diptera), but a hanging fly (Order *Mecoptera*, family *Bittacidae*). *Bittacidae* commonly known as hanging scorpion fly, because of the its scorpion-like tail. It is a long legged predator with an elongated head and a slender mandibulate mouthparts. Here is where I found the difference. Those of the *Bittacidae* are good for pricking other smaller insect, like those of the Robber Flies. The one I had photographed has a much longer beak which I suspect would buckle if it is used to prick other insect. For pricking other insects, the beak has to have a broader base and sharper end. Its slender legs do not seems powerful enough to haul other insects or grasp them.

My suspicion was allayed by Alex from Arizona University. He said, "Nice photo. It is certainly a dipteran, not a *mecop*. In particular, it looks an awful lot like a fungus gnat, *Mycetophilidae*) - the elongated coxae and antennae certainly point it in that direction." Another day, I got this from Pjotr, again suggesting it to be a *Lygistorrhinidae*, this was ruled out earlier due to their geographical distribution. He said, "Your fly is not *Lampromyia* (this genus has very different antennae) but a member of the Diptera family *Lygistorrhinidae*. This was formerly included in the *Mycetophilidae* (Fungus gnats). *Lygistorrhinidae* is a small mainly tropical family with only some 20 described species. The larvae and the biology is little known and the adults are extremely rare in collections." There seems to be discrepancy in the geographical distribution of *Lygistorrhinidae*. I searched the web and found Heikki Hippa of Swedish Museum of Natural History, who did research on *Lygistorrhinidae*, he confirmed that it is not a *Lygistorrhinidae*. Here is what he said, "It is quite sure that the fly is not a *Lygistorrhinidae*. It may be a *Keroplatidae*, but, unfortunately, I do not know them so well and do not have the necessary literature at hand. You could ask Laszlo Papp. Best wishes." *Keroplatidae* was ruled out by Neal Evenhis. Neal, "I told Chris it was not a *keroplatid* but possibly a new genus of *Mycetophilidae* (I do not know of any with such long mouthparts). However, I am not an expert on that family, but you may try Peter Chandler, who knows these flies better than I do. But I agree with Chris' comment to you that it would be best to see the actual critter, the wing venation and the male naughty bits are the most critical characters and high magnification of the wing is necessary to see critical microscopic hairs on the wing."

His suggestion was beyond me. I started out to take portraiture of arthropods. Trying to photograph them in their natural environment. Trying to see their world. Natural lighting was my only way of shooting. I would not want to lay a finger on them. Furthermore, I am afraid of insect. The first thing I did when I returned home after the photography session, was to get a hot shower, to be thoroughly clean. I would never know if I could destroy something that is rare. Would we ever treasure rare insects as much as Panda? Eventually, I did not take up Neal's suggestion.

I approached Dr. Stephen D. Gaimari, Program Supervisor (Entomology) & Co-Curator, California State Collection of Arthropods, that this fly is a *mycetophilid*. He said, "The second photo is definitely a *mycetophilid*. Not my area of expertise, but the family is clear enough." Øivind Gammelmo echoed the same as Dr. Stephen, "*Mycetophilidae* seems sensible. I would say genus *Gnorsite*...." After all these comparisons, I could still see the disparity between those of *Mycetophilidae* and my photographs. Could it be what *Longristra* had said earlier? It is a mosquito? Probably *culicidae*? It had been 4 weeks since I managed to revisit the Botanic Gardens. The delay was partly due to work, the monsoon rain, and my skepticism of ever finding it again. The first day I went, I was disappointed that I could not find any trace of the fly. However, I was rewarded with another rare find, the *Leptogastrinae* (robber fly). It was a good substitute too. Initially, I thought this could be the male of the same insect, but I was proven wrong the next time I revisited the palms. I saw them mating in an amazing position. The female was hanging the male by the genital. So beautiful and awesome! Again they were oblivious to my presence, which was wonderful for me though there was a slight breeze every so often. I was shooting whenever I felt the stillness in the air and they were in focus. It was harder to get both of them in focus as they have to be perfectly in the same plane. Together they measure slightly over two centimeters. There was a noticeable swell at the female bloated abdomen, causing some tearing of the protective outer layer. We will never know whether it was joy or pain during this copulating process. However, we do feel the joy of birth in the making. Nature is so wonderful. I put more photographs into Flickr and continue to search for the identity of my "fly". I have yet to find any photographs of *Gnorsite*. I searched for *mycetophilid*. In Wikipedia, I realized, '*Gnorsite*' was misspelled. It should be '*Gnoriste*'! It was recorded that the family *Mycetophilidae* was found mostly in the fossil Dipter record. They were primitive family. There are more than 3500 described species in the world and many more to be discovered. From the writings on 'Pollination by fungus gnats (Diptera: *Mycetophilidae*)', it was mentioned that *Gnoriste megarrhina* has a body of 7mm long with a proboscis of 6.5mm long which is used to suck diluted nectars from the base of the flora tube. I found something that seems similar. A *Mycetophilid* that does not feed on fungi. This had affirmed my earlier suspicion, it having such a long proboscis. However, I will continue searching.

17. Choosing lenses for macro

I have been quite active in the social networking sites for many years. Most of my work in Flickr is macro work of insects and spiders, occasionally they fall outside this classification, one such instance is Harvestmen, which is considered a rare find for me. Flickr is a great place to learn and foster a close knitted relationship with friends having the same interest. We encourage each other and share our views. I had learned from the many pictures taken by different wonderful photographers. Through their images I learned about their cameras, their lenses and their thoughts. Through them I learned about our similarities, our differences and myself. I had set out to shoot arthropods in existing lights, which set the limits on the kind of images I can capture and the species of arthropods that I can find in bright sunlight. This will exclude those that are active in the night, unless, of course, when the sensitivity of the digital film sensor had improved trememndously.

Often Flickr friends will ask me about choosing the right macro lens for shooting insects. Here is a typical question.

> *"I am about to get into macro shooting so thinking of getting a micro lens. I'm thinking of either the Nikkor 60 mm or 105 mm. May I ask, from your experience, which is a better lens for shooting insects (and other small objects)? What are the advantages and disadvantages of either lens, if any? I'm completely new to micro lenses."*

After shooting for many years, since I was fifteen, looking back, buying the right lens for the right subject is the most important factor in creating that single emotive image. This is even more so for shooting Macro.

I started shooting people and events. Typically, the most commonly used portrait lens is the 105 mm or 85 mm. It was not just because of the sharpness of the lens but the working distance between the model and the photographer that matters. The distance of about a meter keeps the model cool and easy as her personal space is not intruded. Getting too near the model, she will smell the sweat of the photographer. Being too far does not help to improve the intimate relationship between the model and the photographer. It is through the eye and sensitivity of the photographer that brings out the uniqueness of the portraits. For sexy images we can imaging how the model has to flaunt her sensuality before the photographer to reach the final spectators. The understanding of distance will greatly improve the textuality of the image. Of course, the great images always break those rules. You may think that what have that got to do with shooting insects. Let me clarify. Working distance determine the interaction you have with the subject. Insect reacts to lens too. For some insects you will never be able to get within 1 cm away from them, but for some Point & Shoot (PNS) camera, you have to be 1 cm away to achieve maximum magnification. There is always a nearest distance a lens can focus. The photographer will have to develop that comfort zone, moving that comfort zone a few millimetres nearer means a totally new imagery.

I had a lot of interactions with Weaver Ants. When I was too near them they started showing their warring stunt, getting even nearer, they started to open their pincers and snared at me. If I jerked my lens, they would move back abruptly but still ever ready to pick a fight. It is really thrilling to shoot Weaver Ants' portraiture. They are ever reactive and evocative in their bodily expression.

Comfortable working distance

I started with the 100 mm Canon and later I bought the 60 mm Macro. Recently I bought the 35 mm Macro lens. After going through all the 3 different lenses and using that to shoot macros, I realized their pros and cons, apart from their optics characteristics such as sharpness and aberration, working distance is very important.

First I would consider ease of getting near the insect, the 100 mm does a better job as the distance between you and the insect is at a comfortable distance. The distance between the lens and the insect is further with the 100 mm then the 60 mm when you are at the 1:1 magnification but still within a distance where you could reach for subject. However your body and head will be further away from the insect as compared to the 60 mm. The 180 mm would be too far for you to have some form of interaction with the insects or spider. With the 180 mm you are always the remote observer, non-participatory. There is always this fear and inhibition when getting too near the insect, you will be cautious towards the unfamiliar, of course there would always be the few who are the dare devil. So for this first reason I would recommend the 100 mm for the starter.

Depth of Field

This is a very complicated subject. The control of depth of field is really, to me, more visual than scientific. Firstly, Depth of Field (DoF) depends on the focal length of the lens; the longer the lens the narrower the depth of field with other factors being constant. Secondly, DoF depends on the distance between the subject and the lens, the narrower this distance the shallower the DoF. Thirdly, the larger the aperture the shallower the DoF. Of course the one last factor is how perpendicular is the lens with the picture plane. This is why Lensbaby can create selective focus by titling the lens and the picture plane. As the 100mm is longer than the 60 mm, at the same distance and same aperture the image will have a shallow depth of field. However, the image magnification will not be the same. Hence if the magnification is the same it is really difficult to say for sure which have the shallow depth of field, as the degree of impact due to these reasons is difficult to quantify. I had not found a definite answer for the same magnification at the same aperture, which lens has a better depth of field. It could be possible that they are the same. Anyway, for me, I love bokeh and shallow depth of field as I am all for selective focusing and chasing after that portraiture of the minute world. Strangely I have this feeling that I get a deeper depth of field with the 100 mm lens. It is nothing scientific but just an observation. May be someone can tell me whether my feeling is accurate.

This was shot with the 35mm Macro mounted on the Limix G1

Compression of image

When the focal length of the lens is longer, the image appears more compressed. The perception of distance reduces and we tend to misconstrue that the subject is flatter or the distance between the subject and other body is nearer. Cinematographer heightens the danger of a car or alien chasing the earthlings has used this technique. The same happens to the photographing insects and spider. By using a wide angle lens we exaggerate the distance between the subject and us. So when deciding between the 100 mm, 60 mm or the 180 mm, this is major consideration as it determine a compressed or lengthen perspective. Recently, I shot a Cicada with the 35 mm lens; this effect was so obvious that, the Cicada was perceived to be so huge and grand. It made the Cicada so majestic and commanding. So this will depends on the preference of the photographer and his/her style.

This aspect is very personal. Using Flickr is very handy to check the visual impact of wide angle macro or tele-macro. I would recommend that for Macro starters, this is not the most important factor to consider. The difficult of getting near the insect is a major factor. For starter, most have difficulty getting near insects. A longer lens would help, as one can stay further away to achieve maximum magnification.

Lens Size and Angle

As the lens' focal length gets longer, the diameter of the lens barrel gets larger. For sample, the diameter of the macro lens of 180 mm is larger than the 100 mm and the 100 mm is larger than the 60 mm. What is the impact of a larger diameter barrel? It has to do with maneuverability. As the subject could be further away behind bushes, a longer lens barrel with large diameter could be block by branches.

This was shot with the 100mm on 350D

For smaller barrel and reasonable length, it is easier to get good shot of the subject. For the 60 mm, the body is too close to the lens and to move it forward; the whole camera may need to go with the lens including the head of the photographer, if there is no live-view on the camera. The 100 mm could be better off but definitely it is worst for the 180 mm. For the reason of diameter of the barrel, I see the advantage of the Canon 100 mm macro over the Nikon 100 mm. With the anti-shake capability of the Nikon 100 mm the barrel bloated up.

Weight of the lens

I cannot speak for others, but I am definitely one of those who like to travel light and stick to a few fix focal length lens rather than buy up every single lens that is in the market just to collect them or every single zoom I had tried the 100 mm Nikon and the weight when compared to my Canon body plus the 100 mm is much heavier and one would feel the weight after half an hour into photographing the insects.

Anti-shake lens

One advantage of the Nikon Macro lens is the feature of anti-shake or VR (Vibration Reduction), it boast that it can improve hand held timing to lower shutter speed without noticeable blurriness in the photographs. However, I am no so sure about this feature, haven't used a Nikon Macro lens myself. Some had argued fervently that for Macro photography, Anti-Stake does no improvement to the photograph.

Aperture

I had tried the 105 mm Nikkor and realized something strange. Whenever I get close to 1:1 magnification, the aperture reduces to smaller than f2.8. I am not so sure what happens, but I did read a web site confirming my observation and said the lens is a variable aperture lens.

Too Little Action

I can only conclude that if you were selecting between the 2 different lenses, it would be wise to test it out personally or do property peeping in Flickr to see the range of images they both had created. One can get a sense of the lens visual capability and uniqueness.

There will always be differences between different lenses and different brand of camera. All the technical comparison will have to stop somewhere and get on to photographing the micro-world, otherwise there is just too much talk and too little action.

What I did after shooting, was studying the images carefully, investigating the uniqueness of the images created by the camera and the lens. Different camera body with the same lens also performs differently and this is reflected in the image itself. However, the creation of artwork and that special artistic work style depends little on the equipment one uses, but one's creativity and the acceptance of the audience. The best was to adhere to one's believe and one's vision, couple with relentless hard work and unceasing search for the limits of the vision.

18. End

My shots are always happy and romantic perhaps I am always optimistic and it leaks into the camera through my holding hand.

Limitation reveals a particular sensitivity. Liberates the concealed and made the presence felt.

No matter how real the image, it is still an abstraction – inescapable.

Watching the micro world is like watching a silent movie – quiet. Silent is perhaps golden.

Where is the eternal quality of the insects and spiders that would have that power that continuously lure and fascinates the viewers? An image is a slice of time, which the viewer can take all the time he wants to scrutinize and glaze over every pixel that was recorded. Inadequacy, fault, mis-opportunity, and the possibilities the image presents are at the mercy of the viewers, the active critics, or the connoisseurs. They replay, zoom in, zoom out, analyze, associate, recall and introspect, cross referencing the image with their prejudices, preferences, and experiences, possibly reflecting the key to understand life and the universe. How to make an image lasts? I call it the classic quality that never goes out of fashion that can withstand the test of time and has a life of its own.

After the photograph is made and the photographer is gone, it stand only on trial.

This book stand before you, the reader.

About Choo Meng Foo

Meng Foo has been a photographer since he was fifteen years old. At Sixteen he won the Best Print (Student Section) for Asian Salon competition and his work had been exhibited in the Singapore National Museum and the National University of Singapore.
Most recently his work was featured in Asian Geographic, Silverlining, Wave and One magazine. He has been giving seminars and workshops on photography and digital photoshop technique. He has keen interest in shooting theatrical performances, cityscape and Arthropods. Some of his work have been collected in Singapore and abroad.

He was trained as an architect and urban designer, travelled extensively in Southeast Asia. He also love to write, paint, design and think. At 47 he decided to follow the publishing revolution, put his thought into printed books and ebooks. He will require all the support you can render. Thank You.

He can be reached at choomengfoo@gmail.com or zhutianyun@hotmail.com

www.ingramcontent.com/pod-product-compliance
Ingram Content Group UK Ltd.
Pitfield, Milton Keynes, MK11 3LW, UK
UKHW041936190726
13854UKWH00004B/1620